1998

# Changing
# Schools
# from the
# Inside Out

**HOW TO ORDER THIS BOOK**

BY PHONE: 800-233-9936 or 717-291-5609, 8AM–5PM Eastern Time

BY FAX: 717-295-4538

BY MAIL: Order Department
Technomic Publishing Company, Inc.
851 New Holland Avenue, Box 3535
Lancaster, PA 17604, U.S.A.

BY CREDIT CARD: American Express, VISA, MasterCard

# Changing Schools from the Inside Out

### ROBERT L. LARSON
College of Education and Social Services
The University of Vermont

TECHNOMIC
PUBLISHING CO., INC.
LANCASTER · BASEL

# Changing Schools from the Inside Out

a **TECHNOMIC**® publication

*Published in the Western Hemisphere by*
Technomic Publishing Company, Inc.
851 New Holland Avenue
Box 3535
Lancaster, Pennsylvania 17604 U.S.A.

*Distributed in the Rest of the World by*
Technomic Publishing AG

Printed in the United States of America
10  9  8  7  6  5  4  3  2

Main entry under title:
    Changing Schools from the Inside Out

A Technomic Publishing Company book
Bibliography: p. 140
Includes index p. 151

Library of Congress Card No. 91-68578
ISBN No. 87762-901-3

*To Karin,*
*Kimberly, and Jonathan*

# Contents

# Foreword

This book by Bob Larson is overdue reading for anyone interested in truly changing American education. Let me qualify "anyone interested" by defining that as anyone who has been around long enough to see innovations come around for the second or third time. I've lived long enough to go through several cycles of merit pay, two cycles of differentiated staffing (now called career ladders), technology in the form of teaching machines and now computers, democratic administration (now called site-based management), flexible scheduling (now known as open block scheduling), empowerment (once known as involvement and democratic administration and supervision, or the "principalless" school if one were in a militant teacher union), strategic planning (once known as PPBS), behavioral objectives (now called outcomes-based education), and ungraded or non-graded schools. In fact, when one reads about restructuring schools to become more "sensitive" to students and teachers, it is hard to find a whole lot wrong with John Dewey's lab school at the University of Chicago in the early twentieth century.

Now that the politicians have bumped the professional educators out of the driver's seat in sponsoring quick "fix-its" for American schools to outgain the Japanese in the twenty-first century, we are subjected to a rash of mandates and "calls for reform" with each gubernatorial or national election. The brooms sweep in and out. One wave of legislated or executive "reform" is followed by another and another, each as ignorant as the one before, and each spending taxpayer dollars as though they were authorized investment bankers turning a quick deal for profits.

Bob Larson's book is an antidote to this parade of nostrums and the never ending morality play called "in search of educational excellence."

Bob's premise is that change is going on all the time, particularly in "good" schools. It is often unrecognized and unheralded because it is "natural," i.e., it just happens as people in schools look for better ways to do things. In turn, they make the changes necessary without a thought of cash incentives or glory. Effective organizations are changing all the time. They are more fluid than anyone could have guessed merely looking at the brick and mortar from the outside. Larson goes into schools and examines how they change from the inside. What he finds should be comforting to those who want to understand how to implement lasting change and get off the latest education bandwagon with the most contemporary version of "snake oil" cures for poor school performance on tests and other measures.

Larson has defined a data base and a model that won't endear him to politicians who want to get elected or re-elected on the basis of instant prescriptions for educational problems. But he will earn praise from those tired of the never ending cycles of the same solutions with new names for old solutions, and the squandering of public monies to glorify the egos of the few at the expense of true educational improvement.

John Gardner, in his book *On Leadership* (1991, New York: The Free Press), points out that change agents should not assume that organizations are implacable foes of change and therefore make enemies where none exist. Notes Gardner, ". . . In the normal struggles of institutional life one always has friends in the garrison. . . . Why storm the fortress until one learns whether allies inside will open the gates?" (p. 145).

Those who learn the lessons Bob Larson has to teach will find that in the process of changing schools, he or she has many friends in the garrison anxious to help who have already been engaged in changing them from the inside. They will welcome your interest and your energy in assisting the natural change processes already at work in schools.

I've known Bob since 1977 when we met at the National Conference of Professors of Educational Administration at the University of Oregon in Eugene. This book began percolating in those days, when he began to have doubts about conventional views of grand-scale change popular then and now in some quarters. While this book was born of healthy skepticism, I think it is conversely a great source of hope for educators, parents, citizens, and policymakers who want to understand change processes at work in their schools even if they do relatively little to encourage them. When there is understanding and encouragement, these natural processes can expand and gather momentum to cause bigger changes. That is the message Bob Larson brings from his research in Vermont, which connects nicely to national studies of schools. It is a lesson for the rest of America to learn from this New England educator.

Fenwick W. English
*Department of Administration and Supervision*
*University of Kentucky*

# Preface

This is a time of great hope and challenge for public schools. As we approach the twenty-first century, they remain vital instruments for enabling the United States to remain an influential force in the world and for enabling its people to become competent, caring, and responsible citizens.

But this is also a time when their historic nature and mission is being questioned again, and, in some instances, attacked by politicians and special interest groups. These critics would divert already tight public and private resources away from public schools toward alternative avenues of education. In addition, severe budget cuts; uncooperative parents, children, and youth; antagonistic communities; and increased expectations heaped on the organization to address a myriad of social needs are all examples of forces currently pressing on public schools while they struggle simultaneously to increase the quality and relevance of curricula and to become more effective instructionally.

In this context, educators have a great responsibility to seek new opportunities to improve the institution, and to be innovative. The job will be tougher than ever, but we who believe in public education have no choice because it is threatened as never before. We are a key to the future of our young people and to the type of society in which they will live.

Hence this book is dedicated to the thousands of educators and citizen soldiers who help them out there on the firing line, working each day to make schools better and to provide an excellent education for America's children and youth.

As is the case with any venture of this sort, I owe intellectual debts to many individuals. The early ones go back to my doctoral days at Boston University in the mid-1960s when interactions with faculty members Kenneth Benne and Robert Chin (who were two of the early researchers and writers about change), Loren Downey, Stuart Marshall, and Raymond Ostrander began to pique my interest in how organizations adapt to new needs, so too did my involvement as a student with one of the first U.S. Office of Education supported research and training projects on educational change, COPED (Cooperative Project for Educational Development), which stimulated my dissertation study.

During that time I had the good fortune to become friends with the late J. Lloyd Trump, then with the National Association of Secondary School Principals. Lloyd was the model of a careful thinker, an idealist with a vision of a better form of secondary education but one without illusions regarding the difficulty of implementing it, and a down-to-earth school-man all rolled into one. His writings and my experiences with his and the NASSP's Administrative Internship and Model Schools Projects provided me with valuable first-hand knowledge about the dynamics of school improvement. "The Trump Plan," as his overall vision and proposals were often labeled, has had a great influence on altering practices in secondary schools; today's middle school movement is rooted in his ideas.

More recently, I am indebted to several people who have had a hand in the completion of this book. Although it is risky to list names because someone might be skipped, I will venture out on that proverbial limb.

The principals, teachers, and staff at Fair Haven Union High School and the Haven Union School provided the foundational data for half of the pages that follow. They demonstrated a high degree of profes-sionalism in supporting the project, in offering their enthusiastic cooperation and help, and in being candid and thoughtful research subjects.

Robert Arns, then Vice President for Academic Affairs at the Univer-sity of Vermont and now a Professor of Physics, gave me countless hours of time in the early stages of sorting through the theory relative to "garbage can decision making" and "loose coupling" so that we could see what it looked like in practice. He then critiqued the next to final versions of several chapters. My colleague Perry Johnston put the manuscript under his conceptual microscope, from which emerged important feedback that affected the entire volume. George Voland provided expert editorial review, thus sharpening and polishing each page.

My secretary Diana Dubuque doesn't want to count the many messy, "cut and paste" pre-computer drafts that she deciphered and put into readable form. These, combined with her creative schematics of rough pencil sketches, were instrumental to the final product. Robert "Shamms" Mortier of University Media Services also created some schematics from my verbal portraits and reshaped others. Jane Hennessey of the Department of Social Work was my Word Perfect tutor as I launched into composing the book with the new technology. She patiently and cheerfully shepherded me through all the inevitable valleys one falls into and was also available to rescue me by phone during the day, evening, or weekend. Throughout the entire adventure I only "lost" three pages!

At critical junctures, I benefitted greatly from affirming correspondence with Gene Hall, Shirley Hord, Matthew Miles, and James March who also forwarded useful papers. Shirley had a major hand in refining Chapter 6. They are wonderful examples of noted, busy people who always find time to help others in the academy—without delay!

I must add a word about Fenwick English and the crew at Technomic. A few years ago, Fen saw potential in my ideas and recommended my getting a contract to develop them further. His support and encouragement have been constant, with his periodic prods yanking me out of the keyboard doldrums. And Joe Eckenrode, Susan Farmer, and Leo Motter have been exemplars of what a publishing staff should be. Despite my falling behind the target dates, they never applied pressure but instead gave plenty of reinforcement and cooperation to nudge me along on the lonely, yet exciting road of creating a book.

Finally, my thanks to the "home team" of my wife Karin, son Jonathan, and daughter Kimberly. Their understanding, patience, and support for this project, which at times I am certain they doubted would ever appear in hard- or softcover with an ISBN number, will forever be appreciated. To them and to all others mentioned here, I hope that *Changing Schools from the Inside Out* measures up to their expectations.

# Introduction

> Given the relative stability of organizations, one might expect that innovation would be very rare. On the contrary, innovation is going on all the time in almost every organization. [Rogers, 1983, p. 349]

This is a book focused primarily on small-scale change in high schools. It is a book about being successful at incremental, evolutionary improvement by using what works in good schools. What works should also, in most cases, be very applicable to elementary and middle level organizations whether they are in an urban, rural, or suburban setting.

For thirty years, I have worked in and with public schools as a high school teacher, consultant, and professor instructing graduate students, providing service to schools, and conducting research in the field. These experiences have convinced me of the validity of Rogers' assertion. I am impressed by the inventiveness of educators and the adaptability of most of their organizations when it comes to adopting, developing, and dropping innovations within the context of recurring cycles of societal expectations and support for schools.

However, not everyone agrees with this assertion. To many critics that same organization, and particularly the secondary school, is a static and unresponsive institution. Witness, for instance, the spate of recent reports and studies calling again for its redesign, reform, or restructuring. As Powell, Farrar, and Cohen (1985) note, "High school criticism plainly has become a national pastime since World War II" (p. 280). Without doubt there is validity to a lot of the observations of these critics. Without doubt there are many schools that need to be "fixed" in fundamental ways if they are to serve, even minimally, the youth they are charged to educate. Four current examples provide illustrations of such situations.

The first is Rochester, N.Y., where a citywide effort is currently underway to reform schools, K-12. The effort involves installing a site-based management system, altering student-teacher relationships, involving businesses and the community in the schools, linking schools with area colleges, creating new instructional programs, and implementing a teacher contract that allows some salaries to reach $70,000 (*U.S News and World Report*, January 18, 1988, pp. 60-65; June 20, 1988, pp. 58-63; June 26, 1989, pp. 58-60; December 24, 1990, pp. 52-56).

The second example is in Kentucky, where sweeping change is underway, stimulated by a state supreme court decision about the poor quality of education statewide. The Reform Act has mandated the creation of such changes as state-funded preschools for certain at-risk children and children with handicaps; family resource centers for elementary schools impacted by poverty conditions; an ungraded primary school program; school building councils composed of teachers, parents, and administrators; and a guaranteed minimum per-pupil spending level (Walker, 1990, pp. 1, 34-35; *NEA Today*, October 1990, pp. 4-5; Steffy, 1989).

The third is Jersey City, N.J., where the state has assumed control of the system on the grounds that it is "academically bankrupt and rife with corruption, mismanagement, and patronage" (*The Boston Globe*, October 5, 1989, p. 3). This is the only case of actual state takeover of an entire district, a takeover that has enabled the state to appoint its own superintendent, abolish the local board, and select other members of the management team (Olson, October 3, 1990, pp. 1, 20-21).

Finally, there is the unique, ten-year agreement entered into in November 1988 (with the approval of the legislature and governor) between the Chelsea, Massachusetts public schools and Boston University. Distressed by the difficulties the schools were having in meeting the needs of children and youth within a community situation of tangible poverty along with all of its accompanying social ills, the citizens and school board asked the university's School of Education for assistance. Thus the district is currently run by the university under the oversight of the school board (Botsford, 1989).

However, these examples notwithstanding, parents, students, and educators in countless communities are basically satisfied with the quality and form of curriculum and instruction offered by their schools. Such "satisfying" schools, as Goodlad describes them in his landmark study of 38 schools and 1,016 classrooms, ". . . are at a stage of greater readiness for more fundamental improvement" (Goodlad, 1984, p. 270). These institutions, several of which were high schools, are similar to those described by Lightfoot in her popular book about "good" high schools (1983). And the U.S. Office of Education, under a program that is still in operation, between 1983 and 1985 recognized 571 secondary schools as being "unusually successful schools" (Wilson and Corcoran, 1988, p. xi).

This book focuses on these types of organizations. In it, I ask questions such as what can be learned about the dynamics of change in these secondary schools? How can already good schools, or ones that are borderline good, become even better by building on their success?

Such matters are timely, considering the current call to restructure education by starting with the local school rather than (as in the past) emphasizing mandated, across-the-board policies either at the district or state levels, external incentives to change through various grant programs, or planned, "top-down" comprehensive change across an organization or system.

This book has three major objectives. First, it aims to enlarge the knowledge base about planned and naturally recurring small-scale change in the site-managed building—"small wins," to use Weick's (1984) term. This commonplace type of innovation traditionally has been slighted in studies of societies and organizations (Barnett, 1953). Attention to this level of change is needed because the bulk of the literature focuses on planned, systemwide, or sometimes subsystem innovation. A large body of instructive research on this subject is already available to anyone interested in reading it. What educators need more of are resources that can help them to appreciate, understand, and implement smaller scale innovations that can be equally important routes to improving schools.

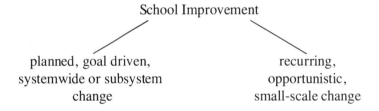

School Improvement

planned, goal driven, systemwide or subsystem change

recurring, opportunistic, small-scale change

Second, this book attempts to provide educators with simple operational concepts and practical techniques that will allow them to become better at effecting and managing change within the hectic, pressured environment of schools. I have learned from my experiences in education the wisdom of the admonition, "Keep It Simple, Stupid!" —KISS for short—which was a major theme in Peters and Waterman's best-selling book, *In Search of Excellence: Lessons from America's Best-Run Companies* (1982, p. 63). KISS and effective change go hand-in-hand; one of the most important contributions made by Peters and Waterman was to make simplicity respectable again.

This is not to say that becoming better at school improvement through more "simple," isolated strategies is an atheoretical enterprise. Indeed it is not. In today's fast-moving organizational worlds, the old dictum "There is nothing so practical as good theory" holds more truth than ever. We must develop our ability to conceptualize and understand the processes associated with small-scale change.

Therefore, the book's third objective is to assist the reader in developing or refining her or his theory of changing. A theory of changing leads to an integration of concepts with technical knowledge and human relations skills, all of which can be concentrated on understanding situations and the factors that might be altered to effect change. Because most change situations involve a number of interacting variables, it is impossible to try to identify and work with each; instead, a way of thinking about change offers the best hope to be of assistance to busy practitioners (Fullan, 1982, pp. 88-100). Toward this end, in the pages that follow readers will find some new applications of old theory and some new applications of new theory.

Readers will also find that this book has more of an organizational/sociological rather than a psychological bent. A significant impediment to improving schools is that educators are reared on preservice programs that are grounded primarily in psychological rather than in organizational/sociological principles. This is understandable, given that the roles for which we are prepared initially have to focus on the student to be instructed; there is virtually no space in undergraduate programs to insert organizational material. And even if the content could be inserted, most undergraduates are far more concerned about and interested in what will happen when they step into a classroom, working directly with students, than they are about stepping into the school's social system.

Consider the thorough preparation in organizational/sociological principles received by undergraduates in a school of business. Compare such a background with that of school administrators who assume their roles with little or no academic knowledge about organizational processes like power, conflict, leadership, communications, and change.

These administrators, however, are expected to lead and manage a cadre of professionals who know equally little about these processes and about the social psychology of living and working in an organization. I have observed countless cases where this mutual "institutional illiteracy" has become the rock upon which many well-intentioned people with good ideas have floundered.

Several themes permeate this book, themes that forthcoming chapters will connect to organizational literature. They provide a conceptual framework for *Changing Schools from the Inside Out.*

- Organizations are always changing, but usually in routine, fairly unnoticed, rather than in dramatic, heroic ways.
- Change is usually effected by ordinary people doing ordinary things in a competent way.
- Routine organizational processes are often key levers for improvement.
- Change occurs in an often unpredictable and not well-understood fashion.
- Organizational adaptation is an interplay of rationality and foolishness, of cognition and affect.
- Small wins can set in motion a process for continued small wins—a process that strengthens organizational capacity and ability to solve larger-scale problems.

Schools can and do change, but oftentimes the ways in which they improve, as is the case for all organizations that are effective, are relatively imperceptible, and are far from headline-grabbing. These subtle changes, however, are instrumental in making schools better. This book will provide some additional tools for the school improvement kits of administrators, teachers, other school personnel, and board members who are struggling every day, against great odds, to educate our youth.

# The Current Context for School Improvement

A democracy demands of its education both quantity and quality. Never before have so many been educated so well as in the United States. These achievements have been the result of constant efforts to experiment, spurred by the desire to improve. The challenge of quantity has largely been met. Most of America's youth are in school and most classrooms have teachers. But the challenge of quality is now more difficult to meet than ever before. [Trump, 1959, p. 5]

As we move toward the twenty-first century, we enter a decade of turbulence and challenge on the national and international scenes. In one form or another, we Americans and most others in the global community will continue to experience the phenomenon of future shock as first predicted by Toffler in 1970. As I complete this chapter in early 1991, the euphoria of a year ago when the Iron Curtain began to fall has given way to an increasing sense of apprehension as events in Eastern Europe cloud the hopes for democracy and market economies, as the aftershocks of the Gulf War continue to reverberate across the Middle East, and as our national economy becomes mired in a recession.

Because of worldwide communications systems, rapid intercontinental air travel, and the availability of miniaturized media, virtually no part of the globe can expect immunity from jarring events like these, no matter how remote and traditionally isolated from the mainstream of current industrial or emerging postindustrial society. Daily newspaper and television headlines shout confirmation that the old order is changing, whether or not we want it to.

The 1990s will be a transition decade as we find ourselves caught up in other megatrends relating to a global economy, new forms of free-market socialism, privatization of the welfare state, the rise of Pacific Rim powers, women in leadership, and religious revivals (Naisbitt and Aburdene, 1990). Toffler, who has written three influential books about the future (1970, 1980, 1990), contends that we are now experiencing vast shifts in traditional forms of societal power as the industrial system undergoes radical change within the United States and around the world.

1

Old economic theories, models of industrial development, and ways of measuring economic and social progress are no longer guideposts to a predictably better future. At the heart of these shifts is a new system for creating wealth that is bound up in the new information and communication technology.

Accompanying these changes will be accelerating shifts of a less measurable kind. We feel these shifts already, for at times it seems like virtually every mainstream attitude and value is under siege from some quarter. Technological advancements force consequences on people's lives that their proponents seldom, if ever, considered before the "advancement" was implemented. Until the mid-twentieth century, individuals and social institutions like the family, church, and school generally adapted to the technology because the technology itself did not arrive with its current destabilizing power.

Change usually spawns more change, but traditionally it was evolutionary and gradual in its impact. Today, most of the time, that is no longer true. Different family patterns, genetic engineering, fertility control, prenatal surgery, determining where life begins, prolonging life, invasion of privacy, living and dying with AIDS, new lifestyles and sexual mores, sex roles, the work ethic, mind-expanding drugs, artificial life, and earth's survival, limits to growth and political, social, and economic upheavals in many nations are but a few of the significant forces and issues now clashing with conventional attitudes and values.

Cornish (1990) notes that "human problems have proliferated at an accelerating rate in the twentieth century, so the 1990s will likely be the most worry-filled decade that mankind has ever experienced" (p. 29). On the other hand, the very fact that there are so many problems is, from Cornish's point of view, an indication of progress because as we learn more and develop responses to problems, we discover what does not work, we discover more things to be concerned about, and, in turn, create more solutions.

## EDUCATION AND SOCIETAL CHANGE

Schools are caught in this web of societal change. The impact of it on curriculum, instruction, and learning is significant but not always understood clearly.

In addition, in the United States, there is general agreement that we are fast becoming an information society, a society where knowledge is the primary industry, where it is valued more than traditional labor, and where it is the driving force affecting our future. In Bell's words,

> Broadly speaking, if industrial society is based on machine technology, post-industrial society is shaped by an intellectual technology. And if capital and labor are the major structural features of industrial society, information and knowledge are those of the post-industrial society. [1973, xiii]

When the graduates of the class of 2000 leave high school, knowledge will have doubled four times since they began their education in 1988. They will have been exposed to more information in that year than their grandparents were exposed to in their lifetimes. But they will enter an American marketplace that will require a college background for only 15 percent of jobs, and where minorities will be majorities in fifty-three of our 100 largest cities (Cetron, 1988, p. 10).

Educators, in addition to being wrapped in a blanket of complexities and perplexities thrust on them by societal change, find themselves caught up once again in a wave of educational reform that began in 1983 with the publication of *A Nation at Risk* by the National Commission on Educational Excellence (1983). That document galvanized the attention of the nation with its sharp criticism of the condition of public education and its rhetoric about the threat to our economic future posed by that condition. ''We have in effect,'' the Commission said, ''been committing an act of unthinking, unilateral disarmament'' (p. 3).

These critics, and ones associated with other reports, singled out the high school as the key culprit. High schools, they said, must change if we are to insure our economic and political viability in a world where it is no longer a given that the United States will be the dominant power.

Political response to these concerns has been rapid and sweeping. For example, since 1983 states have generated more educational rules and regulations than they enacted in the previous twenty years, and between 1984 and 1986 they passed more than 700 statutes affecting directly or indirectly some dimension of public schooling (Timar and Kirp, 1989). Most of these statutes fall into four categories: higher academic standards for students; recognition of the importance of the role of the teacher; ways to reward teachers for superior work; and higher standards to enter the profession (Passow, 1989, p. 17).

These reforms fit the category of what Cuban has labeled ''first-order'' changes, those that aid in improving the effectiveness of what schools do now. They are not aimed at bringing about ''second-order'' reform, reforms that will inject new goals or perhaps alter the fundamental goals of education, that will alter the ways in which schools are organized, and that will alter the ways in which traditional roles are performed within the organization (1988, pp. 341-344). Currently the "restructuring" movement (discussed in Chapter 7) is, in the eyes of most of those promoting it, an effort to cause second-order change at all levels of public schooling.

Cuban's conceptualization of change captures the central, age-old tension that confronts schools and educators—the role of the organization as an agent of change rather than as a pillar of the status quo.

The school as an agent of change was President Johnson's vision when, in his education message to Congress in 1965 recommending the passage of the Elementary and Secondary Education Act, he said,

> We are now embarked on another venture to put the American dream to work meeting the new demands for a new day. Once again we must start where men who would improve their society have always known they must begin—with an education system restudied, reinforced, and revitalized. [*N.Y. Times*, January 13, 1965, p. 20]

Then millions of dollars were appropriated to enable education to take on the tasks of societal improvement. During the 1960s the federal government was supporting the broad goals of achieving excellence and equity.

In contrast, President Bush's vision of reform, spelled out at the 1989 "Education Summit" with the nation's governors, revolves around "competitiveness, improving the learning environment, accountability, flexibility, tougher standards, and a result-oriented system" (Cohen, 1989, p. 18). These goals are first-order and are rooted in themes of efficiency and effectiveness.

A reading of the goals statement adopted by the National Governor's Association demonstrates that the six goals, although very important, reflect more of a present than a future perspective. They do not address matters of societal reform. Rather, the goals address children's readiness for elementary school, increasing the high school graduation rate, increased competency in basic curricular subjects, adult literacy, and drug- and violence-free schools. "These goals are about excellence" (National Governors' Association, 1990, p. 16).

But they are also goals without significant additional funds to promote their achievement. The President's proposed budgetary increases for education, although more than proposed by former President Reagan, lag far behind what Congress has proposed for the current fiscal year (Olson and Miller, 1991, p. 30).

Also, the October 1990 federal deficit reduction legislation includes spending caps in three broad categories – domestic, military, and foreign aid. Under the law, funds cut in military spending, for example, cannot be shifted to support domestic programs. Such cuts would apply to reducing the deficit. Any increases in domestic spending would have to come from like programs. Congress, under the law, has, in turn, ceded considerable power over the budget to the administration's Office of Management and Budget (Rasky, 1990, pp. 1, 22).

It is clear that one of the prime goals of the Reagan administration has been achieved: to reduce significantly the federal government's role as underwriter of major expenditures for education at state and local levels.

## PAYING THE FREIGHT

Although many states and communities have expended immense funds in the 1980s to replace lost federal dollars in order to implement their various ''top-down'' reforms or to promote improvements, projected costs in these regards are staggering.

For example, an early attempt to estimate funds needed for the nation's 15,885 school districts to implement most of the recommendations in *A Nation at Risk* concluded that their 1982-83 budgets would have to be increased by at least $21 billion. In 1981-82, the total operating budgets for these districts was $106 billion. To implement only the recommendations to raise teacher salaries and to lengthen the school day and year would, in 1982-83, amount to $60 billion (Toch, 1983, p. 1, 19). In Vermont in 1984, while legislators and educators were debating proposed new state standards for elementary and secondary education (since implemented) the then-Commissioner of Education estimated that it would cost districts nearly $16 million to comply (Peck, 1984, p. 1B, 4B). Said one local board member, ''You can't argue with the standards, but where will the money come from?'' (Powell, 1984, p. 1A).

Given projections for climbing enrollments in the nineties – enrollments that will require at least a 5 percent increase in real expenditures just to stay even – the '' new game'' will be to find any other monies for school improvement at the state and local levels (Sirkin, 1985, p. 6).

Unless there is an about-face in the financial fortunes of most states, such monies will not likely become available. Although most states enjoyed economic health into the mid-1980s and could thus fund enacted improvements, the economic tide has receded, leaving massive deficits in at least thirty states that block attempts at school reform (Tye, 1990, pp. 1, 38-40).

A January 1991 survey of the states resulted in a dismal economic outlook for the next couple of years, at least. More than half the states will have to make cuts in current budgets or postpone spending to balance current budgets. Governors and legislators were cited as saying that the prospects for new educational reform initiatives or increased aid to schools "are dim or nonexistent." Some had doubts that basic aid programs could be maintained (Harp, 1991, pp. 22, 24-25).

Vermont is an example of a state in this kind of economic fix. In the spring of 1991, 32 of 174 proposed budgets were defeated at town meeting time. Subsequently, fifteen were defeated twice, and nine districts went to a third vote. The defeats in 1990 were a 45 percent increase over the defeats in 1989 (Geggis, 1990, p. 1B). In all likelihood, according to the Commissioner of Education, increases in state aid to education for fiscal year 1992 will be below the rate of inflation (*The Burlington Free Press*, 1991, p. 2B).

## DOING BETTER WITH WHAT WE HAVE

J. Lloyd Trump, the inventor of the "Trump Plan" to change patterns of curriculum and instruction and the overall structure of the secondary school (e.g., large group, small group, individualized instruction, flexible scheduling, and differentiated staffing) had a favorite slogan: "Doing better with what you have" (Trump and Georgiades, 1970, p. 106). In the decade ahead this will need to be the placard on everyone's desk. Although additional monies may be forthcoming to some local schools from federal and state governments, and although some local municipalities may have the resources to support significant large-scale reform, there is little doubt that overall resources in the nineties will be "thin" when it comes to extra funding for such activities. Educators are once again faced with a condition that emerges periodically with the bull and bear market moves of the economy.

The situation today will challenge our creativity, patience, and energy, for we will have to learn, as Michael Kirst suggests, "how to improve schools without spending more money" (1982, pp. 6-8). He contends that considerable improvement has occurred in elementary and secondary education during hard times, but it has tended to be of the simple and not eye-catching sort—the introduction of the Carnegie unit of instruction at the turn of this century, for example, which although initially being of "low cost," has had a tremendous impact on curriculum and instruction. Kirst sees a return to the emphasis on "alterable variables" such as time, curriculum content, instructional methods and materials, and teacher quality as the focus for improvement.

Bloom similarly would place more emphasis on such variables, emphasizing those relating most closely to learners and learning. He contends that we are at a juncture in educational history where we can have a great impact on the quality of education by focusing more of our efforts on using what we know from research about these variables (1980, pp. 382-384).

## REFORM AND REALITY

Kirst and Bloom identify some of the basic changes that educators know will improve schools. Most of these changes, however, are evolutionary, not revolutionary in nature. They do not square with the more ambitious expectations for change through the "reform-through-policy" strategy that has been the focus at the federal level since 1960. This policy route has had two thrusts: one was to create more equity in the schools through programs like Title I combined with civil rights legislation, and the second was to stimulate excellence through programs such as Titles III and IV-C and NSF curriculum grants. Elmore and McLaughlin, in the Rand Corporation study of those reform efforts, state that this approach is grounded in two assumptions: (1) there are some basic defects in the overall system of education that can be corrected by implementing some specific policies, and (2) these will result in better classroom practices that will have more national uniformity, which, in turn, will be supported and maintained by administrators and organizational structures.

But, as the authors state, "In reality, reform is more like the process of introducing changes into a language. Language is independent of our efforts to change it" (p. 13). Gradually, as more and more words are added to a language, fairly dramatic differences become apparent, as can be illustrated by the contrasts between Elizabethan and modern

American English. However, English is still English just as a school is still a school. Elmore and McLaughlin go on to observe that ''school systems respond to external pressure for change, not by highly visible, well-specified, sequential actions, but by subtle shifts over time'' (p. 13).

From the perspective of most citizens, the schools from which they graduated are the same as they were years ago. Although the identical observation could be made about virtually any social institution, schools face a particularly unique situation: virtually all citizens have been members of the organization for a significant portion of their lives. By the time they finish high school they have observed about 15,000 hours of classroom teaching, a powerful experience that shapes their lifetime image of schooling. Hence the first-order changes that have occurred and that continue to be implemented in good schools remain virtually invisible to the layperson, the legislator, and the would-be reformer.

To the school critic, a top-heavy administrative hierarchy and a cadre of unimaginative, change-killing teachers seem the prime reasons why the organization is fixed on the status quo (Sarason, 1983, pp. 13-14). This is often the point of view of the reformers described by Elmore and McLaughlin. Such reformers usually have learned few lessons from the history of prior reform efforts and instead tend to place the blame for resistance to change at the doorstep of school personnel. These conclusions are similar to a major one that emerged from Goodlad's research: ''We refuse to face the realities of what it takes to change such complex social/political institutions as schools'' (Tye and Tye, 1984, p. 319).

On the other hand, a considerable number of other critics see things quite differently. To them, schools tend to be mindlessly faddish, jumping regularly on the latest innovation bandwagon. Educators are viewed as passive, malleable people, all too inclined to adopt the latest promoted panacea. From this perspective, rather than not changing enough, the more important problem facing schools is their tendency to change too much (Sarason, 1983, pp. 15-16).

## ORGANIZATIONAL DILEMMAS

As with most perspectives, there is an element of ''truth'' in each. Some organizations appear static; others appear adaptable. ''Nothing happens there,'' some observers say about some schools. ''That's an innovative organization,'' they say about another.

In some schools, such as those in Rochester, Kentucky, Jersey City, and Chelsea, conditions have deteriorated so much and a maintenance orientation to education has become so dominant that it takes concerted, external action to get improvements. These organizations have not found ways to deal satisfactorily with the basic organizational tensions or dilemmas that confront all social institutions. They have been unable to establish processes through which to address the issue of when and how much to change (Miles, 1981, pp. 104-110; Katz and Kahn, 1978, pp. 770-771). They have been unable to focus their resources and energies on their prime educational tasks rather than on bureaucratic needs and political survival, and they have been unable to figure out how dependent they should be on their immediate external environments for clues to new directions (Miles, 1981, pp. 57-82).

However, whether or not they resolve the dilemmas, they will change. Every organization changes. Accompanying change are issues relating to the extent that change is intentional on the part of organization members or pushed on the organization by other forces, the types of innovations, their shape and size, whether they are adopted or developed, and the degree to which they connect to one another and to the mission of the organization.

## ACTION WITHIN AND AROUND THE CONSTRAINTS

As professionals, it is incumbent on us to be knowledgeable about the context within which schools function, the current forces causing change, and the ongoing dilemmas they face. Although the discussion so far has focused on the broad societal level regarding schools, in a very real way the concepts are directly applicable to local buildings because each operates within a social context and is confronted with tensions relating to change.

A school can decide by intent or by default to be a passive structure and allow the context, forces, and dilemmas to work themselves out, carrying the organization in some direction. As poorly as it might perform it will still survive; it will not go out of business under current rules.

Conversely, the school can decide to be a more causative agent and act on the context, forces, and dilemmas within the narrow window of action available to it. According to Cuban, who conducted an extensive study of how high school teachers have taught since 1890, that window is the classroom. "The most promising place to begin is precisely where the resources should be concentrated: the classroom teacher" (Cuban, 1982, p. 117). To veteran educators this conclusion is far from startling. It reaffirms what we have always known to be the key to school improvement—an excellent curriculum delivered effectively by the teacher in the classroom. But the policymakers and the critics continue to ignore this "bottom-line" to reform (Cuban, 1984, p. 260).

Classrooms, of course, are not isolated entities. They exist within the structure of the school itself, and more specifically to this book, the high school. That school has again become the focus of reform efforts, just as it was in the 1960s when Trump and his associates were writing about new designs for it (Trump, 1959; Trump and Baynham, 1961; Trump, 1977), and James Bryant Conant was reporting on his studies of the same organization (Conant, 1959; 1967). For years Goodlad has pointed to the school at all levels as the unit for educational change (1984, pp. 31, 271-279). Now his message is being listened to intently and acted on in the form of the site-managed school, which will be discussed in Chapter 4.

Before the local school received the attention it is getting today, however, various approaches were taken to effect needed changes in education. Chapter 3 will present an overview of these approaches, including highlights of major studies conducted regarding change and innovation.

# Notes on Change from Research and Practice

> The image of innovation shattering a serene status quo is particularly inappropriate in the modern world. Given the tumultuous sweep of technological and social change, there is no serenity to shatter. The solutions of today will be out of date tomorrow; the system in equilibrium today will be thrown out of balance tomorrow. [Gardner, 1990, p. 125]

Formal study of change processes and the factors that affect them in public schools began in the late 1930s, with Mort and Cornell's groundbreaking analyses of the spread of innovations in Pennsylvania school districts. These innovations included such things as kindergarten, extracurricular activities, supplementary reading, and a reorganized high school (Ross, 1958, pp. 31-51). These kinds of innovations were "big" in size and scope in that they were seen as being adopted across entire school systems. From these influential studies emerged the "lag theory" — that most schools are slow to adopt substantive innovations, taking an average of fifty years to do so after the practices have been employed by the first users or "lighthouse" schools.

But Mort and his associates found that increased financial support could reduce significantly that time frame. Such support produced quicker results because, for example, (1) schools could more deliberately assess their needs and make themselves knowledgeable about new practices to meet those needs; (2) they could hire a staff of well-prepared, capable teachers, including teachers who might become "spark-plugs" for the innovation; and (3) they could hire administrators who valued innovation, knew how to work with a staff to bring it about, and who did not allow the management dimensions of the job to co-opt the responsibility for effecting change (Ross, 1958, pp. 407-496). As we shall see, these factors are similar to many of those that current research tells us are critical to successful change.

In addition, the Mort group identified a general process of adopting innovations. Briefly, it encompassed these steps:

11

(1) Recognize a need and articulate it.

(2) Propose a solution.

(3) Arouse interest in it.

(4) Have a trial demonstration.

(5) Increase support for it.

(6) Officially recognize the innovation and obtain financial support for it.

These steps were a precursor to many rationalistic change processes that were developed in the years following Sputnik in 1957.

Aside from three decades of valuable field studies and the publication of several monographs connected to the initial work of Mort and Cornell, no publication of note about change in schools emerged until Miles' *Innovation in Education*. This 1964 book discussed various kinds of change processes and innovative practices in the late 1950s and early 1960s. Since Miles' work, the pace of publications has increased steadily so that today there is a voluminous and instructive amount of literature available. Hence, just as we now possess considerable useful knowledge about subjects like effective teaching and effective schools that can guide professional practice, we now have detailed knowledge about planned change and innovation at the level of the school district and school.

## CHANGE AND INNOVATION

Although the terms *change* and *innovation* are used virtually synonymously in the literature, they have distinct meanings that are important to note here. Change may occur whether willed or not, whether planned or not, due to forces both within and outside the organization. Change can range in magnitude from simple alteration or substitution of practices to the levels of restructuring ideas and systems and adopting new values.

Innovation, on the other hand, is typically thought of as the intentional act of introducing something new into a situation. Deliberateness is at the heart of innovation. Change can be accidental. An innovation is always a change, but a change is not always an innovation.

Beyond mere definition, however, is the fact that while persons who introduce an innovation may perceive it as novel and unique in that situation, the innovation may not be so new to the realm of practice. This notion that innovation is very situationally defined is common to the literature (e.g., Hall and Hord, 1987, p. 9).

It is easy to get entangled in a definitional tug of war. Although writers tend to use these terms interchangeably [and I will take the advice of Rogers and Rogers (1976, p. 153) and do so in this book because the patterns and processes connected to each are so similar], the conceptual differences are evident. The ability of the school to adapt to new needs and demands rests largely upon its innovativeness.

## ADAPTABILITY

Adaptability in education is usually thought of as ". . . the capacity of a school to take on newer and more appropriate educational practices" (Mort, cited in Ross, 1958, p. 26). The concept was integral to the early research on school improvement.

While the word, to some people, may imply simply reacting to events — adjusting accordingly — its use in the organizational literature is intended to imply acting before the organization is compelled to do so by the myriad of forces that swirl around every social institution. Intentionality, rather than crises, would set direction. Failure to adapt would deprive the school of the influence it should have over its future, and its programs would become increasingly outmoded in relation to the needs of its clientele.

Although many organizational theorists have contended that adaptability is central to any organization's long-term health and effectiveness (e.g., Schein, 1980, p. 35), the concept has not received much attention in education during the last three decades of research on change and innovation. The most noted exception has been John Goodlad who, in his various writings, has promoted the idea of the self-renewing school. Given external pressures for schools to change quickly, it is likely that adaptability has not gained headlines because it is an evolutionary route to improvement, and that route bumps up against the impatience of policymakers and many lay people.

Since the publication of the Peters and Waterman book in 1982, however, adaptability has become respectable again as a key characteristic of a healthy and effective organization. That volume catapulted innovation to the top of corporate America's agenda. Readers began to recognize that ongoing change, sometimes on a very small scale and often at an imperceptible level, was crucial to the survival of a business in today's turbulent marketplace. Change in these organizations has come to be viewed as expected; it becomes the norm rather than the exception.

Kanter, who has studied such private sector environments, puts it this way:

> It is this kind of company that can more readily produce the adaptive response which helps an organization stay ahead of change, shifting posture and resources as circumstances require. It is this kind of company that stimulates and empowers its people to innovate. [1983, p. 130]

In other words, innovation does not always have to be splashy or sweeping in order to be important.

## FORMS OF CHANGE

Thus far the discussion has conveyed the message that the organization has a choice to change or not to change. However, in addition to voluntary action, schools change due to osmotic and policy forces. Although these three forms of change — osmotic, policy, and voluntary — are, for discussion purposes, separated here, to many readers the distinctions may appear to be problematic. It is often difficult to decide exactly which one was the root stimulus for a particular innovation. Regardless, it is instructive to recognize the three broad forms of educational change portrayed in Figure 2.1.

### Osmotic

Many times change just "happens" or seems to "creep in" to the organization. It is unclear where it originated or who was responsible for initiating it locally. The osmotic process demonstrates how bound the school is to the evolution of the larger society, since forces connected to this society often give educators little choice but to adopt, develop, or jettison innovations.

For example, student attire and deportment are considerably different today than they were in 1958 when I began to teach high school. I recall standing at the cafeteria door to inspect boys' boots and girls' hemlines. But a societal shift occurred and dress codes disappeared — with the assistance of the courts — and my school and others found themselves powerless to resist the change. Currently — and just as osmotically — dress codes are enjoying a revival as society pressures schools to

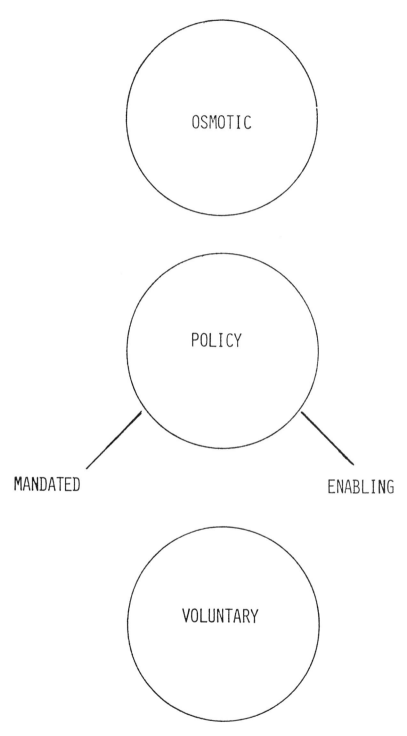

**Figure 2.1** Forms of Change.

establish more order in the face of an increased number of unruly students and public criticism about the lack of internal control.

Another example of the osmotic process is the swing between ''back to basics,'' ''open education,'' and ''humanizing the school.'' Right after Sputnik in 1958, we witnessed an emphasis on basic education. Then, in reaction to Vietnam, our racial upheavals, and a general feeling that schools were placing too much emphasis on traditional knowledge at the expense of attitudes, values, and feelings, humanistic education became the focus. Society returned to the basics in the mid-1970s in reaction to the perceived excesses of humanistic and open education.

Societal changes of all kinds cause '' innovative'' responses in schools. In shaping this chapter, I began to clip from newspapers and news magazines relevant articles and columns relating to education. I was astounded at the drawer full of material that I collected. The seemingly endless demands on schools clash with proposals for a more focused curriculum, the most noted being a central tenet of the Coalition for Essential Schools that ''less is more'' for the regular curriculum (Sizer, 1984, pp. 109-115). In other cases, the ''services curriculum,'' which deals with social and psychological needs (Powell, Farrar, and Cohen, 1985, pp. 33-39), is expanding and siphoning resources from the academic curriculum. Society continues to pile more expectations onto schools and expects schools to make room for them in the curriculum.

In terms of the regular curriculum, here are some examples of the osmotic process at work. In response to the AIDS epidemic, more explicit sex education units are being added. In response to environmental issues, a ''fourth R'' −recycling− is being infused into the curriculum. In response to the danger of guns in homes, some schools have implemented ''gun awareness'' units. In response to drug and alcohol problems, more material on these subjects is being appended to curriculum at all levels. In response to a stressful environment at home and at school, some organizations have developed ''stress management'' courses. In response to an influx of new immigrants, schools are having to create more ''English as a Second Language'' experiences. In response to efforts to reduce the dropout rate, new relationships are being forged with business and industry that will lead to different work/study programs. In other cases, alternative schools have been created for this at-risk population.

In terms of the services curriculum, here are some examples of the process at work. In response to ''no pass, no play'' policies in districts or at the state level, special tutoring programs are developed. In response to disruptive or distressing home situations, many schools have created new counseling programs and support groups for students and parents. In response to health care needs, new relationships have been formed with social service agencies that offer services in the building. In response to working parents, some schools have installed early morning and late afternoon study hall/recreational programs. In response to working teenagers, some schools have had to alter homework practices.

The growing pressure to add services has been demonstrated to me vividly during the past two years while attending my local district's budget hearings. I live in a "typical" suburban community, which has adequate resources and which has always supported its schools. There are few children on free or reduced lunch arrangements, and Chapter I services are minimal. Yet I have observed a decided trend whereby the elementary principals (in this instance) are requesting more help through additional nurse and nurse's aide time to deal with children who are often left ill at school because working parents cannot stay home to care for them, and more counselor time so that counselors can give additional attention to children of divorce and blended family situations, provide crisis intervention services, and offer parent counseling and parent support groups. As one of the principals put it,

> Families are having lots of difficulties. The needs keep increasing. When you see a child who's fighting all the time, has no friends, and is just kind of down and out, you have to respond.

In responding to these needs, there has consequently been minimal increase in the budget for regular programs over the last two years.

The dynamics of this osmotic process (although not labeled as such by the authors) have been described in depth in three volumes written by Smith, Dwyer, Prunty, and Kleine (1986, 1987, 1988). They sketch the evolution of the Milford School District over sixty-five years and examine how the changing community affected innovation in the Kensington Elementary School over a fifteen-year period. At one point in their study they conclude,

> Furthermore, we find that many of these changes are not Milford or Kensington innovations, that is, planned, creative changes initiated by the District of the School. Rather they are reactions and responses to factors originating in these multiple, external contexts. [1988, p. 266]

A major impact of the force of the surrounding environment on the school was the fact that in a decade and a half it went from being one of the most innovative to being one of the most traditional organizations in the district.

Society evolves, writers write, commissions issue reports, commentators talk, and parents raise questions (sometimes). Educators then react, either trying to fend off the changes they see and feel, or adapting to them. If one is ahistorical or lacking in understanding about the school as a social institution, this osmotic process may be greeted with considerable cynicism, reinforcing the image that most educators will jump mindlessly on the latest curricular or instructional bandwagon. On the other hand, if one places the process in context, these oscillations are understandable, ''normal,'' and to be expected as the school tries to fulfill its twin roles as an agent of cultural transmission and an agent of change. To the astute educator, what worked yesterday, but was then discontinued, may work again today in a different situation with a new group of students. What may appear to be a fad may be a good solution to tomorrow's new/old problem. The societal pendulum swings and schools move to its rhythm.

## Policy

In contrast to the osmotic process, many changes are imposed on schools, or schools are induced to change. Such ''mandated'' and ''enabling'' approaches stem from policies enacted at the federal, state, and local levels (adapted from McDonnell and Elmore, 1987).

### Mandated Change

Schools must comply with laws, regulations, and court decisions. Those who are mandating contend that the law in question was necessary because the organization had failed to address a certain problem. In most cases, there is considerable evidence to support that assertion. But mandates stir lots of emotional and value reactions that can lead to endless debates about the need for the directive and its positive or negative impact on the intended outcome.

An old but still useful example of radical mandated change is Public Law 94-142, the Education for All Handicapped Children Act which, from the day it was enacted in 1975, has had a significant influence on curriculum, instruction, values, and finances.

Since 1983, as described by Timar and Kirp in Chapter 1, states have enacted more rules and regulations about education at the local level than they had in the previous twenty years, and between 1984 and 1986 passed close to 700 statutes.

In Vermont, Act 230 of the General Assembly (1990), a statewide policy effective July 1991, is having a real impact on curriculum and instruction, grades K-12. Under the law — sometimes referred to as a regular education initiative — extra resources will be infused into the system to limit the inappropriate use of special education. These resources will be used to train teachers and support personnel themselves to work with mildly, moderately, and severely handicapped children and youth in regular classrooms. Instructional support teams, composed of a majority of teachers along with proportional representation of the rest of the professional staff in each building, will have a key role in screening students and determining what resources and training are needed to serve them. The major goal of Act 230 is to enable more children to have their academic and behavioral needs met in regular classroom settings.

This mandate occurred because there was an increasing feeling among educators and many advocate groups that it was the "right thing to do" to integrate these children and youth into regular classrooms rather than to keep them relatively separate from their peer groups. Also, observation showed that special students were too isolated socially and that too often present instructional practices were not effective. Finally, policymakers at the local district and state levels were concluding that some other approach had to be tried to educate all special students because the current practice of providing education to them was too expensive. As one District Special Education Coordinator put it recently, "We had to try something."

A standard form of mandate is the high school accreditation report or the state education department assessment of local schools. Schools must address the recommendations made through these assessments or incur a penalty.

Title IX of 1975 is an example of an affirmative action mandate relating to discrimination against women in the workplace and in schools. Regarding the latter, it has caused significant changes in curriculum content, participation in sports programs, and reallocation of financial resources.

Fundamental to mandated change is rationalization, the assumption that there is a clear and direct connection between means and ends, between the laws, regulations, and policies on one hand, and certain goals on the other. The managerial processes of organizing, directing, and evaluating illustrate the concept of rationalization.

Sometimes the link between means and ends seems clear. But, as Wise contends in an incisive analysis of contemporary policy-making (by federal and state governments, the courts, and the executive branches), we are in an era where ". . . we are witnessing the phenomenon of hyperrationalization—that is, an effort to rationalize beyond the bounds of knowledge" (1979, p. 65). This approach often leads to outcomes such as excessive prescription, procedural complexity, and the application of inappropriate solutions to problems.

Ten years later Wise still sees strong evidence of these effects stemming from more recent state efforts to gain more control over the schools (Wise, 1988). These outcomes, combined with the complex nature of the school as an organization (to be discussed in Chapter 3), lead to ineffective policy implementation that, combined with the societal shifts discussed earlier, leads to drawing on prior solutions (sometimes in modified form) that previously had worked or not worked (Cuban, 1988).

### Enabling Change

This form of policy uses the metaphorical carrot (usually money) to induce change. Its aim is to improve schools by providing additional resources that will, in turn, increase the innovative capacity of the organization. Enabling policy fits well with the idea of adaptability or the self-renewing school.

The 1950s, 1960s, and early 1970s were the heyday of funding to stimulate change. Then NSF monies flowed to support projects in developing new content in most subject fields and new approaches to delivering that content. Federal dollars were also available to support the reeducation of teachers. Title III provided grants to local districts to develop innovative practices, and later Title IV-C allowed state education departments to allocate monies to schools to stimulate change. Mixed in with these sources were immense sums from private foundations such as Carnegie, Danforth, and Ford.

But today things are different in relation to enabling policy. The tight financial situation across the country, discussed earlier, has caused a radical shrinkage in all kinds of funds now available to induce innovation at the local level. As we saw in Chapter 1, in most states "the money just isn't there." Although the federal government underwrites the National Diffusion Network, support to adopt and implement innovations from that system is the responsibility of the local district.

## Voluntary Change

While policy change either directs or induces change from outside, voluntary change emerges from within the organization. The school decides to initiate the change, or decides to participate in it. In some cases the organization may adapt something forced onto it, it may choose to adopt an innovation, or it may develop its own practices or processes.

Consider again the example of "back to basics." It illustrates the crossover that sometimes occurs between the three forms of change discussed in this section. The "back to basics" movement may lead to state or local-district mandates, and these might usher in different types of voluntary innovations to address the needs identified in the mandate. This is common practice in many states where great programmatic latitude is given to local districts to invent their own ways to comply with state regulations.

Finally, the organization can take a compliance stance where it does only the minimum to fulfill the requirements of the policy. Instead of finding ways to use the mandate to improve education, the attitude is, "Just do what we have to do and soon those bureaucrats will be off our backs!"

### *Adaptation, Adoption, and Development*

These three concepts are integral to voluntary innovation. One major criterion of a healthy organization, as we saw earlier in this chapter, is its adaptability, and the hallmark of adaptability is the organization's ability to initiate change — to innovate. When we examine Bromley and Mansfield high schools, we will look closely at the dynamics of this process.

Presently, the National Diffusion Network's menu of validated innovations is a prime example of a source of adopted change. These programs, designed by educators in the field, come in all shapes and sizes, as can be seen by reading the 1990 edition of "Educational Programs That Work." Peer supervision, adult literacy, student writing, diagnostic prescriptive arithmetic, and team learning are examples of the 400 tested innovations available to schools. Given limited time, resources, and in some cases a scarcity of inventive personnel, it is often very sensible for an organization to search for and adopt innovations from elsewhere, provided that the local context is analyzed to insure a good match between program and setting.

Because NDN programs are judged to be "valid," however, local adaptation of innovations is discouraged due to the possibility of lessening program impact. Studies show that success can be attained with this "fidelity" strategy, but that the road to success can be very rocky (*Educational Leadership,* November 1983; Huberman and Miles, 1984).

There are times, however, when adapting an adopted innovation is the best route, given the local context. The Rand study of federal programs supporting change (outlined further in Chapter 4), showed that when schools are engaged in a process of "mutual adaptation" — modifying the innovation to fit the realities of the institutional setting — success can often result. Such "learning-by-doing" takes time, much participation and patience, and effective leadership on the part of those directing the effort (Berman and McLaughlin, p. 28). A major consideration that needs highlighting here is the fact that the programs studied by the Rand researchers (e.g., bilingual education, vocational/career education, and reading) were initially not well-defined, in contrast to the NDN options, and therefore virtually required adaptation if they were to be implemented and maintained well rather than discarded. However, this research also demonstrated the difficulty schools had in attaining success through adoption/adaptation.

Alternatively, a district or school may innovate by fashioning a defined program, which meets local needs, out of related elements that have not before been connected into a set approach. This "mosaic strategy" (to be discussed in Chapter 7), slightly different in emphasis from the one studied by Rand, also demands lots of time, skill, and energy.

An illustration of this route to improvement is provided by the Model Schools Project of the National Association of Secondary School Principals. This Project, conceived by the late J. Lloyd Trump and initiated in 1969, was the most ambitious effort to date to bring about comprehensive change in secondary schools — to restructure them. The thirty junior and senior high schools that participated committed themselves to installing an organization-wide model of improvement that included team teaching; differentiated staffing; flexible scheduling; learning activity packages; new roles for administrators, teachers, and counselors; and various methods to individualize instruction. These components of the model, although defined fairly specifically, could be joined together and implemented in ways deemed best by the local school. When the project ended officially in 1975, research indicated a checkered pattern of success in the organizations involved (Trump and Georgiades, 1977; *NASSP Bulletin*, November 1977).

The Rural Experimental Schools Program is another example of a development strategy that met with few successes. It was a federal program that provided funds for five years to support comprehensive change across a district at all levels. Seed money was provided for districts to develop innovative programs that would lead to school improvement, programs that ranged from new curricula, psychological services, community involvement, and program evaluation, to individualized and diagnostic instruction. Research findings demonstrated that, overall, these changes had little positive impact in the districts and that, in many instances, they also caused serious internal disruption (Herriott and Gross, 1979).

An illustration of a more successful application of this comprehensive strategy is John Goodlad's 1966-71 League of Cooperating Schools project. In it, eighteen elementary and intermediate schools joined together to find ways to become ''self renewing'' through cooperative problem solving, shared resources, and planned interventions to increase the probability of successful change. When the project was formally over, researchers identified eleven of the eighteen organizations as having become better at collaborative problem solving and change as a result of their involvement in the League (Bentzen et al., 1974, pp. 153-169).

## LEVELS OF CHANGE

Three levels of change are common in organizations: system, subsystem, and individual (Figure 2.2).

In education, the system might consist of the district or the school; the subsystem might be the school, the department, or program; and the individual, the teacher. Most research has focused on change across districts and schools. This book focuses on departments, programs, and individuals.

**Figure 2.2** Levels of Change.

At all levels, a number of variables exist and they interact in numerous and often confounding ways. It is tempting to think that change is more "simple" at the level of the individual, but that is far from true. As we will see in Chapters 4 and 5, "micro" personal variables such as values, abilities, motivation, and relations with peers and supervisors play a major role in one's reactions to change. Then, as one works up the system ladder, other organizational variables are added such as power and authority, communications, decision making, leadership, incentives and rewards, resources, and rules and regulations.

This "layering" of variables contributes greatly to the confounding nature of change. One day, in one setting, it seems simple and relatively easy to implement an innovation. Another day, in another setting, that same innovation seems maddeningly difficult to attain with the most well-planned and sophisticated of efforts. Conversely, in the place where the innovation was not too difficult to effect, a few weeks later walls of resistance may appear in relation to another change.

The impact of understanding or not understanding how these variables affect change was identified by Huberman and Miles (1984) in their detailed field research about the adoption or development of National Diffusion Network and Title IV-C innovations in twelve schools. They found that administrators lived in different institutional worlds from teachers, tending at first to see the innovations as relatively simple and straightforward to use and having the potential to result in considerable organizational improvement.

Teachers, on the other hand, saw the innovations as complex, inherently ambiguous, and difficult to use. They were skeptical about the potential for real change. In general, eventual successful implementation hinged heavily on administrator recognition of teacher views of the innovation, understanding of the processes associated with their use, and administrative assistance to overcome or minimize impediments.

Wolcott, in a study of one district's attempt to install, "top-down," a programmed budgeting system, identified great differences in how teachers perceived and reacted to this "macro" level change contrasted to the way that the "technocrats" (the administrators) viewed it (1977).

Other research on district or organization change (cited earlier) gives testimony to the power of these variables to block or diminish the intended effects of innovations. As Fullan said, after an exhaustive analysis of the literature, ". . . Planned change attempts rarely succeed as intended" (1982, p. 6).

This is not to say that there is no evidence of successful planned change efforts. As we have seen, there were many ''good news'' stories from the National Diffusion Network and Title IV-C sites and Goodlad's schools. And Vickery has written about the implementation of Outcomes Based Instruction in Johnson City, N.Y., which is now the only district-wide ''exemplary program'' in the current NDN catalog (Vickery, 1988; 1990). But results from all the research fall largely on the formidable side of the ledger.

Where more research is needed is at the level of small-scale change. Perhaps more has not been done because innovations at this level appear not to cause real change; they typically do not involve basic alterations in professional role conceptions and behavior—important indicators as to whether there is real versus superficial change—and such change may not make much of a difference in the educational process (Fullan, 1982, pp. 31, 59). Huberman and Miles have similar views about small-scale innovation (1984, p. 186).

These arguments are persuasive, but we cannot put schooling on hold or jump over existing situations while we debate and conduct more research on change and innovation at more ambitious levels. Instead we need to appreciate small-scale approaches as important avenues to improvement. We need to find ways to make this level of change more potent for organizational renewal. However, this type of innovation occurs within a complex organization, the school, and a complex component of the school, the classroom. Both are the focus of Chapter 3.

# Schools as Organizations

> There are, in the school, complex rituals of personal relation-
> ships, a set of folkways, mores, and irrational sanctions, a moral
> code based upon them. There are games, which are sublimated
> wars, teams, and an elaborate set of ceremonies concerning
> them. There are traditions and traditionalists waging their world-
> old battle against innovations. [Waller, 1965, p. 103]

While the society around them becomes increasingly complex, most schools appear to their external critics to be tidy bureaucracies that are relatively simple to manage and to change. Perhaps this is because, as was discussed earlier, most citizens have spent several years in the organization, directly observing teaching and experiencing its rituals, folkways, mores, sanctions, and ceremonies. Thus there is little mystique to the education profession, and self-proclaimed experts in curriculum, instruction, and learning abound in every community.

Added to their ranks are those successful as teachers who staff religious education programs and local community organizations. In sum, classroom teaching, according to popular misconception, is straightforward and relatively easy work: a teacher simply pours knowledge into the heads of students.

Each of us wears a pair of socio-psychological glasses through which we see the education process and the organization within which it takes place. We identify patterns and we make interpretations. We come to believe in our perspective. If the perspective is somewhat accurate regarding the realities of the setting and accompanying phenomena, then we conclude that it is wise to maintain our investment in it. If the perspective proves to be inaccurate, however, we need to change our glasses or we will continue to bump against reality and against those with a clearer understanding of the dynamics of the workplace.

## THREE PERSPECTIVES ON CHANGE

House describes three perspectives on educational change: the technical, political, and cultural (1981, pp. 17-41). The *technical perspective* emphasizes rationality of behavior. To attain organizational goals, one must establish bureaucratic structures and processes to promote hierarchical control and suppress competing interests and values. Then the route to improvement can be a fairly clear means-ends route – one that emphasizes an effective technology leading to an identifiable product.

In terms of change, this perspective may focus on the innovation that often emerges from a research and development process and that should work in any setting where it is implemented (e.g., National Diffusion Network innovations, provided there is a good match with the situation). Or it may focus on the process of planning, which can be treated in a highly technical fashion. Whatever the focus, it assumes that rational people ought to adopt a tested innovation on its merits or that the outcomes from a well-outlined planning process ought to be implemented and used.

The *political perspective* emphasizes that there is seldom one route to achieve goals. Issues of power and authority permeate every human setting, and therefore there is often conflict over what the goals should be and how they should be achieved. Cooperation among groups is not automatic; one must often resort to negotiation and compromise to set a direction, and even then forces inside and outside of the organization may redirect energy and affect outcomes. A critical element in this mix is the impact of the external environment.

With regard to change, this perspective focuses on processes to work through issues of power, authority, and conflicting values. But because of all the give and take, the final shape of the planning process itself or its outcomes, or the shape of an innovation, may not please all parties. However, once things have been agreed to, there should be "fidelity" to the use of any adopted plan or innovation. Mort's studies, discussed in Chapter 2, reflect dimensions of the technical and political perspectives.

The third perspective, *the cultural*, is getting more emphasis today as a way to understand organizational change. Its roots can be traced to Waller's classic study, *The Sociology of Teaching*, written in 1932. It underscores the importance of the particular context in terms of the shared elements of norms, beliefs, and values held by individuals and groups of participants (e.g., administrators and teachers) in that context. Each individual and group derives "meaning" about change through those elements. Wolcott's (1977) previously cited research on a rational planning and budgeting process in an Oregon school district portrays vividly the deep gaps of understanding and meaning between "technocrats" (administrators) and teachers that can submarine a technically well designed innovation.

All individuals in a school work within such groups (for teachers, other subgroups might be defined by grade level or by subject area such as social studies and mathematics). The respective norms, beliefs, and values of these groups may differ considerably from those of other groups or from those of the total organization. Shaped slowly over time, these cultural features become guideposts for behavior and tend to preserve the status quo. They may become similar enough so that people can work together fairly effectively, but they can also become magnified so that the organization is rife with conflict, controversy, and resentment.

Hence change, from this perspective, unless imposed, tends to be evolutionary. Innovations are altered as they are implemented—as they sometimes are through the political process—so that they fit better into the local context. Also, group cultures inhibit organization-wide changes but can nurture small-scale improvements.

Each perspective is valuable for giving us greater understanding of organizational change. For example, successes or failures relative to the use of National Diffusion Network innovations, the Rural Experimental Schools Project, or the Rand Study of Federal Programs can be explained by an analysis through the various perspectives, just as Wolcott was able to examine the planned innovation in South Lane.

This book focuses on educational change from a cultural perspective. It does so for two reasons. The first is that this point of view has had far less treatment in the literature, and thus there is a need to expand its knowledge base. The second is that the case studies of the Bromley and Mansfield secondary schools surfaced findings that were far more illuminating in terms of the cultural perspective than in terms of either the technological or political perspectives.


## SCHOOLS AS ORGANIZED ANARCHIES

Although schools possess characteristics common to all organizations —a division of labor, a hierarchy of authority, rules and procedures— they have other characteristics that are not in keeping with the traditional notions of bureaucracy. March and Olsen (1979, pp. 24-93) apply the label "organized anarchy" to these features. In broad terms, organized anarchies lack specific, well-defined, consistent goals; their processes for delivering their service cannot be easily explained; and the participants (in this case educators and students) vary in their involvement in and commitment to the learning enterprise. Organized anarchies are thus rife with uncertainty and ambiguity, cultural features not usually associated with bureaucracy. (What follows is drawn primarily from March and Olsen 1979; Miles, 1965; and Waller, 1965.)

Some characteristics of schools as organized anarchies are

- problematic goals and goal ambiguity
- zero client rejection
- a changing clientele
- fluid participation
- value of experience over research and education
- minimal use of technology
- loose coupling
- high teacher autonomy and low peer visibility
- adults' interaction primarily with children
- low professional mystique
- lay-professional control
- internal and external vulnerability

We will examine these characteristics in more detail.

## Problematic Goals and Goal Ambiguity

Organizational-level and even program-level goals are typically broad and indeterminate — e.g., "develop responsible citizens," "appreciate and know how to use leisure time," or "be adept at mathematical problem solving." Such goals are open to interpretation, so it is difficult to know how to achieve them or how to measure whether they have been learned.

On the other hand, because the school must meet a wide variety of student, parental, and community expectations, broad goals may be the best one can hope for. More precise goals would likely generate conflict between school constituencies because such goals would leave little room to accommodate differing views. Since parent groups change with each entering first grade and exiting twelfth, school goals face continual scrutiny. And each new school board member carries around his/her perception of the meaning of these goals.

## Zero Client Rejection

The school must serve all students, and the mix is becoming increasingly diverse with more special education and at-risk youth in regular classrooms, along with an influx of immigrants from non-English speaking and non-western cultures. How do educators capture the interest of this clientele? How do they manage classrooms of captive audiences whose motivation ranges the spectrum from cooperation to passivity to often vigorous resistance? By accepting all comers, education in a democratic society holds great promise. On the other hand, by doing so in a time of limited resources, the risk of not being able to serve all groups well increases.

## A Changing Clientele

Every year a significant segment of the population changes as older students graduate and a new class enters kindergarten. Those entering include the tractable and eager to learn, as well as the unstable and resistant. For the school each year, it is the luck of the draw. For the teacher on opening day, it is always a new adventure building relationships with individuals and classroom groups. A single strongly reluctant learner or special needs child can require incredible teacher effort if the individual and class are to flourish during the year. Without positive relationships, little of lasting value can be accomplished in the classroom. Clearly, any innovation that upsets or has the potential to upset these human dynamics is quite unwelcome.

## Fluid Participation

Not only do student attitudes toward learning vary considerably, but even students who are generally motivated and interested in education differ in their degrees of participation in school affairs. Young people are tugged in many directions by their peers, their own physical and psychological development, their parents, their personal heroes, and the media. Thus the organization must expend considerable energy to capture and retain the attention of sporadically involved learners.

As is true for any social institution, employees vary in their commitment to organizational goals and involvement in organizational activities. Although the hiring of capable and motivated people can go a long way toward insuring sustained involvement, a less-than-healthy organizational environment can quickly undermine this attitude and behavior.

Finally, the teaching profession is classed by several researchers as a ''semi-profession'' — one that has (1) low entry requirements, (2) relatively low pay and societal status compared to other professions, (3) low organizational level job autonomy (but considerable autonomy within the classroom), (4) a considerable degree of lay control over its affairs, (5) no disciplinary control over peers, (6) the lack of a body of professional knowledge and skill that is perceived as ''special'' by the clients served and other relevant constituent groups, and (7) no differentiation in salary based on performance (Lortie, 1975, pp. 1-24; Lortie, 1969, pp. 1-53). Therefore the organization must expend effort to gain and hold the attention of employees because professional norms and role expectations may not do so.

## Value of Experience over Research and Education

Unlike time-honored professions such as law, medicine, and theology, which are rooted in traditional bodies of knowledge and research, public education is weak in this regard. Despite considerable educational research over many years, it is rare to find enough agreement among researchers on any one finding so that practitioners feel they can, with a high degree of confidence, make decisions based on it.

Therefore, it is difficult to demonstrate to educators that a certain approach to instruction or a certain curriculum is more effective than another. Such decisions are still made primarily on the basis of experience and conventional wisdom. As research on the profession demonstrates, the most valued dimension of teacher education programs is student teaching, not the knowledge base acquired during four years of preparation (Lortie, 1975, pp. 70-74).

This professional ethos also means that it is very difficult to initiate change among administrators or teachers based on research findings. These professionals place more credence in what their experience tells them will work rather than in what research indicates might work.

## Minimal Use of Technology

Schools are ''labor intensive'' organizations. The basic work of the organization is done through people, and despite the introduction of modern technology, social transactions are the major mode of instruction. They are the major mode because interactions with students provide primary rewards to teachers, and (until the advent of the computer) most technology has been too difficult to use on a mass basis or has been too unreliable. Due to their labor intensiveness, an average of three-fourths of most school budgets support personnel, leaving little room to increase effectiveness, efficiency, and productivity through technology. Even if the technology promised effective instruction, teacher unions would likely resist if it meant reductions in force.

## Loose Coupling

Schools are composed of classrooms, but the connections between them are relaxed so that each, even at the same grade level or in the same subject, has its identity and physical separateness. Weick refers to this structural feature as "loose coupling" [1976, pp. 1-19]. Unless operating in a totally dysfunctional fashion, what happens in one classroom rarely has a noticeable impact on another. This structure promotes quick responses by individuals or small groups to small changes in the environment and meets professional needs for autonomy, but impedes implementation and institutionalization of large-scale innovations.

In addition, features of the organization such as zero client rejection and a captive clientele can lead to professional behavior (e.g., relating to discipline) that is loosely connected to school goals. Also, because decisions within this structure may not directly affect many decisions made elsewhere in the organization, it is difficult to assess their impact on others that often appear related. March points out that these phenomena guarantee some degree of "foolishness" within an organization that ought to behave rationally (1981, p. 574).

## High Teacher Autonomy and Low Peer Visibility

In most schools, teachers within classrooms work independent of their colleagues. They teach at the same time as their colleagues; they use break time for preparation rather than for conversations with peers. Teaming arrangements are the exception rather than the custom. The autonomous classroom and logistics of the daily schedule make it almost impossible for teachers to observe each other's performance. Although people work across the corridor or in the next room—whether in a ten-teacher school or one with ten times more staff—they do not see first-hand how colleagues teach nor do they share materials or ideas. This pattern makes it difficult to implement and institutionalize innovations that require staff to work together consistently.

## Adults Interact Primarily with Children

While isolated from their peers, teachers spend most of the day at close quarters with "kids." Despite real efforts on the part of many schools to find ways for teachers to work together more consistently, the structure of the schedule is difficult to alter for such purposes. An elementary teacher put it like this: "I spend most of my day in my classroom with my children. There are days when I don't talk to or see another adult." And a high school teacher said, "It can be emotionally draining to deal with adolescents all day" (Franklin, 1991, p. A25).

Success in the profession stems mainly from successful relationships with one's students, not one's peers. When it comes to considering change, the opinions that matter most to teachers are likely those of their charges, not their peers.

## Low Professional Mystique

Because everyone has been through school, most lay people feel quite familiar with how educators go about their work. This knowledge gives the general citizenry a sense of control that contrasts sharply with the sense of control it feels toward other professions. Therefore educators, to sustain relationships with the public, must listen to its complaints and often entertain seriously the proposed "solutions" to problems made by people outside of the system. Such activity takes time away from other creative endeavors, and helps bolster the misperception that education is anyone's business.

## Lay-Professional Control

School boards govern schools, and although these policymakers have not been served by the organization for years, they carry in their minds an image of education based on their own school experiences. Board members may see themselves as quite "expert"; they may feel they know what the school should or should not do. The organization must listen to them, and in some instances respond to their agendas for innovation because of dynamics in the political environment. Sometimes the agendas may be beneficial and other times not.

Schools sometimes suffer when the lay policymakers try to manage the organization and dictate change in curriculum and instruction. But in some communities, citizens and politicians have concluded that the dismal condition of education or the feeling that they are not welcome in the school requires such involvement. As Snider (1990, p. 11) states, "Tired of being left on the sidelines, a growing number of parents are asserting their voice on school-governance decisions once left solely to educators." Numerous cities have implemented what is commonly referred to as local school councils. These units, often composed of educators, parents, citizens, and students, are given formal authority over organizational matters such as budgeting, curriculum development, selection of instructional materials, and hiring and evaluating personnel. In Chicago, although the arrangement is being challenged in the courts, parents have been given a controlling majority on the councils.

## Internal and External Vulnerability

Because schools are built around children and youth, they are under the constant threat of disruption by the very clientele they serve. In addition, every citizen is a potentially vocal shareholder in the organization (as demonstrated by the school council movement) with an investment that fluctuates—depending on the issues and whether one has a child in school. Beneath it all is another current of vulnerability, caused by the "osmotic" process discussed in the last chapter, a process that subjects the organization to the swings of the social, economic, and political forces surrounding the school.

Glickman and his colleagues have been working on a statewide school improvement project in Georgia. Several demonstration schools have installed teacher-led participatory decision-making processes. Many new programs are in use and a real impact has been made on reducing dropout rates, increasing student achievement in basic subjects, and improving organizational climates. But, as he points out, the overall context that supports such an endeavor conveys no assurance of permanency and stability, so ". . . there is always the feeling that the floor could fall through at any moment" (*Phi Delta Kappan*, 1990, p. 70).

## CLASSROOMS AS BUSY KITCHENS

The classroom is where it finally all happens. It is here that the major formal efforts to teach youth occur. If there is no success at this level there is, for most students, no other place to go to learn. And it is within the classroom that innovations succeed or fail.

Classrooms are, in the view of Huberman, "busy kitchens" (1983). They are a unique type of social system; no other profession is structured so that its service is delivered day after day, in a fairly set routine, to groups rather than to individuals, and groups that are often unwilling clients. Yet within the group the needs of individuals must be met.

In many ways teachers are like chefs, drawing on their recipes and preparing meals each day. They work, as we have seen in the previous section, in relative isolation from other adults. This isolation is not only from peers, but in many instances from supervisors. It is not unusual to hear teachers say, in a course or workshop, that have been working for fifteen or twenty years and have never been observed by any adult.

The following characteristics of teaching are drawn mainly from Jackson, 1968; Lieberman and Miller, 1984; Lortie, 1975; Pellegrin, 1976; Sarason, 1982; and Waller, 1965.

Some features of classrooms as busy kitchens are

- emphasis on psychic rewards
- balancing affect, control, and cognition
- hectic pace, volume, and variety of the work
- presentism, immediacy, and serendipity
- importance of instructional style

We will examine these features in greater detail.

### Emphasis on Psychic Rewards

Although money, prestige, and power are important to teachers, as they are to any professional, most teachers teach for less tangible reasons. Lortie, the most cited researcher on the profession, states, "The structure of teaching rewards, in short, favors emphasis on psychic rewards" (1975, p. 103). What happens for the learner in the classroom is of prime importance to teachers. A twenty-year update of the 1964 data upon which Lortie based his findings resulted in virtually identical conclusions (Kottkamp, Provenza, and Cohn, 1986).

## Balancing Affect, Control, and Cognition

I teach in a university. If I wanted to, I could simply lecture to my students and give them tests. If they learned the material, fine, but if they did not, so be it. I could teach that way and not be concerned about how students felt about me or the material. I would not have to worry about classroom control.

Not so with the public school teacher. To be successful with a captive audience, one has to juggle the dimensions of attitude, feeling, value, classroom control, and what is to be taught. Relationships are critical in establishing order and discipline; without them, not much learning will occur. The teacher has to deal with affect and control before addressing what is to be learned in order to create an environment that can produce learners—and personal psychic rewards.

This juggling act became personalized for me a few years ago when I was on a sabbatical leave studying the Bromley and Mansfield high schools. Because I had not taught public school since 1964, I thought it would be good "reality therapy" for me to do so again. I was correct, and while I found little difference between the past and the present instructing the motivated, college-oriented social studies classes, such was not the case with other groups.

I was jarred by the differences in the attitude and deportment of students in these groups compared to the difficult boys and girls I had taught almost thirty years ago. I expended an immense amount of psychic and physical energy keeping control while trying to build and sustain relationships—and teach them something. Cuban, who also returned to a high school to teach after being in a university setting, came away with similar impressions (1990, pp. 479-482).

## Hectic Pace, Volume, and Variety of the Work

Classrooms are beehives of activity. Place one adult and twenty-five young people within the close quarters of four walls and one has a "busy" situation. Teachers have to facilitate discussion (one study estimates that a teacher engages in at least 1000 interpersonal interchanges each day) (Jackson, 1968, p. ll); formulate a host of on-the-spot questions; assess individual learning; decide what assignments to give; manage the overall use of time; choose expectations to communicate and communicate them effectively; maintain a safe, orderly, and academically focused environment; deal with deviant behavior; and enhance a cooperative group feeling.

This pace continues through the day, six to eight periods in a row for the school year (at the high school level). Typically there are three or four minutes between classes, a free period for planning, an extra duty (study hall monitor, cafeteria or hall supervisor), and a brief lunch break.

On top of these demands, teachers deal with a seemingly endless list of other tasks. Prior to setting foot in the classroom, teachers have to make decisions about content to be taught, the time to be allocated to it, methods to be employed, key questions to ask, how learning is to be assessed, and how to work with certain individuals or groups within the class. Then, when instruction ends, the teacher has to read papers, correct tests, determine grades, and decide the form of feedback to students and when to give it. Berliner, who has studied teacher decision making, has sorted these decisions into pre-instruction, during instruction, climate, and post-instruction categories (1984, pp. 51-75).

The paperwork associated with regular classroom teaching is formidable, wearing, and enormously time-consuming. One study demonstrated that over a seventeen-day period, fifty-eight teachers handled 3893 pieces of paper covering areas from tests to homework to discipline (Freed and Ketchem, 1987, p. 16).

The hectic pace, the volume, and the variety of the work force teachers to create repetitive routines to help them survive amid the swirl of so many variables. Standardization, not diversity, becomes the norm; this survival strategy explains why classrooms look so similar everywhere and why the same patterns of instruction persist in the face of efforts to alter them.

## Presentism, Immediacy, and Serendipity

After my stint "in the trenches," I kept thinking that for the high school teacher, the future is now—at 9:00 or 1:00, whenever the next class arrives; that is the overriding concern. In higher education, the future is often next semester—when we will be instructing that new course; or next summer—when that workshop will be offered; or next year—when that book deadline arrives. By comparison, public school teachers live under the gun.

The immediate need to respond to learners forces teacher energy and interest to focus on the present moment. Jackson's research led him to conclude that ". . . it is today's behavior rather than tomorrow's test that provides the real yardstick for measuring the teacher's progress'' (1968, p. 123).

It is this emphasis on the present, however, that can lead to small-scale innovation, to serendipitous responses to what is happening in the classroom since effective teachers must constantly ''tinker,'' adjusting to unanticipated demands (Huberman, 1983, p. 487). Chapters 4 and 5, describing findings from Bromley and Mansfield, will portray this process.

## Importance of Instructional Style

Teachers develop a very personal style as they aim each day to balance affect, control, and cognition. No one ''formula'' works for all teachers; rather, each instructor undergoes a process of trial and error that often involves considerable pain and distress before he/she begins to find ''what works.'' But what works with one group may not be as successful with another because of the particular mix of personalities and needs. Style is never perfected because each year a new group of students arrives and the process begins again. Considerable energy is diverted from delivering the content per se because of constant pedagogical demands.

The issue of style is critical to change because a teacher will not alter, except for very good reasons, something so personal that has evolved over many years. Style is the ''bottom line,'' so to speak; upsetting it can threaten the pedagogical life of the teacher. Without classroom control nothing is accomplished. Very likely this reality explains why research in secondary schools demonstrates consistently that it is far easier to implement curricular innovations as opposed to instructional ones (Orlosky and Smith, 1972, p. 413; Rutherford and Austin, 1984, p. 54).

## SPECIAL FEATURES OF HIGH SCHOOLS

In addition to the characteristics discussed thus far, high schools possess other characteristics that have implications for effecting change. They are usually fairly large—500, 1000, 2000 pupils—and size affects the way education is delivered. They are usually organized into departments, which further complicates organizational processes because departments reinforce separatism between teachers, and departments focus on their particular subject and on their often conflicting educational goals (e.g., a common stress on affective-type goals among social studies staff and a common stress on academics in mathematics). Cooperation and communication between these subsystems is difficult. Scheduling students into subject areas, along with trying to accommodate levels of ability and involvement in co-curricular activities, results in a complex daily schedule. Students usually only have contact with specific teachers one period a day, and they move through a seven- or eight-period day. This pattern erodes the ability of the school to develop norms of affiliation with a significant segment of its prime clientele, norms that could help to motivate learners.

Because students are older, parents usually express less interest in their children's school activities and thus obtaining parent cooperation and involvement is difficult and time-consuming. Adolescents also carry into the organization a greater variety of needs and attitudinal and value conflicts than do children. This fact, combined with the reality that a higher percentage of them, compared to elementary and middle school youngsters, would rather not be in school, causes considerable professional attention, time, and energy to be allocated to custodial functions at the expense of matters relating to curriculum and instruction.

Secondary schools are also subject to more intense external pressures than other schools. The media, jobs, and peer expectations of recent graduates all compete for student interest. In some communities, expectations for varsity sports play an important role in the life of the organization. Social phenomena associated with drugs, alcohol, and sex have a real impact on a large portion of the student body. Finally, these external forces bring into the organization the effects of community social agency intervention on behalf of many students, intervention that also requires time from educators within the building.

## The Role of the Principal

An axiom of school administration is that the principal is the instructional leader of the organization. Few principals would state that this is not one of their key roles. However, as a new study of the high school principalship reveals, there are many interpretations of the term. For some administrators the role is one that is directly involved with teachers in curriculum development, management, change, and instructional improvement, while for others it is one that addresses primarily the managerial dimensions of the work, all of which, in one way or another, have an impact on curriculum and instruction (Pellicer et al., 1990, pp. 27-41).

Historically, the principal's role has sometimes been defined by the school with the expectation that whoever occupies the office will act in an instructional leadership capacity. Sometimes the role has been left to the principal to define, assuming that she has the ability to act as an instructional leader and/or manager. And sometimes the size of the organization has permitted others (e.g., department chairs and central office staff) to take on these functions.

However, today there is an emerging consensus within the profession and within the society that the principal must take on more instructional leadership functions if schools are to improve. The functions cannot happen by chance. For example, in their 1991 Report on Education, the nation's governors said,

> Strong leaders create strong schools. Research and common sense suggest that administrators can do a great deal to advance school reform. They will lead the next wave of reform, and states and Governors must act now to help them lead. [*Time For Results*, p. 10]

If the principal wishes to be an instructional leader, then research tells us that it is very difficult to act the part (e.g., Gottfredson and Hybl, 1987; Manasse, 1985; Martin and Willower, 1981; Pellicer et al., 1988; 1990). The role is strikingly similar whether it is in an urban, suburban, or rural setting, whether it is in a large-, small-, or medium-sized organization, and whether it is in a high, middle, or elementary school. At the organization level, schools are also "busy kitchens."

Principals' work is characterized by a high volume of activity including a wide variety of tasks that are brief in duration, often interrupted, and often managerial rather than instructional; by tasks that are brief and fragmented so that rarely is there an opportunity to give undivided and sustained attention to any one of them; and by a hectic pace that leaves little room for reflection and planning. As Lieberman and Miller point out, "Educational leadership happens, when it happens at all, within and around the edges of the job as defined and presently constituted" (1984, p. 76).

When combined, do these characteristics of schools and classrooms make change for the better nearly impossible? It often appears that way: the impediments and challenges can seem insurmountable. Such is not always the case, however, as we will see in Chapter 4 when we examine the way good schools can and do improve despite the constraints.

# Bromley and Mansfield:
# Two Case Studies

> Schools will improve slowly, if at all, if reforms are thrust upon them. Rather, the approach having most promise, in my judgment, is one that will seek to cultivate the capacity of schools to deal with their own problems, to become largely self-renewing. [Goodlad, 1984, p. 31]

Given that all schools and classrooms possess the characteristics described in Chapter 3, why is it that some high schools are judged to be "good," "satisfying," or "successful"?

The notion of a "good" school has been around since schools were invented, but it was Lightfoot, in her noted book, who developed the best working definition. She states that "goodness" is a holistic concept, very situationally determined, that includes people, their relationships, their motivation, their goals, and their will. It also includes measurable indicators such as attendance, vandalism, and truancy and aspiration rates (1983, p. 23). Good schools are characterized by norms of cooperation, collaboration, and caring—norms that make the organization a generally pleasant place to work, whether that work is done by the staff or the students. To understand what makes a good school good, one must examine its context through the cultural perspective outlined in Chapter 3.

What Lightfoot does not include in her definition are two other vital factors relating to "goodness." The first is the autonomy to be "site managed"—the practice that has captured the headlines in convention agendas, professional literature, reports from foundations, and speeches from politicians. The second factor is the ability to change, usually in small-scale, unobtrusive ways.

A site-managed school is one in which those who make decisions also implement them (American Association of School Administrators, 1988, p. 5). The schools studied by Lightfoot, by Goodlad (1984), by Wilson and Corcoran (1988), and by Lipsitz (1984) were administered in this way rather than being controlled by a remote, central office.

In addition, evidence shows that these schools adopted or developed small-scale innovations steadily and incrementally, a characteristic, as we saw in Chapter 2, that is essential to organizational health. Academic improvement came mainly through improvement in courses, the prime change-bearing vehicles in high schools (e.g., Lightfoot, pp. 102-110; 196-207; 249-252). Given the single-classroom structure of high schools, such improvements through courses thus consisted primarily of individual staff actions.

So the good news is that considerable innovation occurred in these schools. On the other hand, the authors of *The Shopping Mall High School* (Powell, Farrar, and Cohen, 1985) are critical of this kind of change, along with many changes in co-curricular activities and social and psychological services, because they lack focus in relation to the overall mission of the organization. The authors charge that academic programs are not rigorous enough and that students are given too much freedom of choice. Others contend, as we saw at the conclusion of Chapter 2, that these kinds of changes are not significant and will not lead to substantive educational improvement.

Here we have a conundrum. Most high schools have the ability to innovate in "first-order," small-scale ways, and good schools have even more of that capability. Most students and parents seem quite satisfied with the education provided by these organizations. On the other hand, many critics conclude that these changes do not and will not make much of a difference in terms of the real impact the organization should be making on its students. They assert that we need "second-order," larger-scale, more comprehensive change.

Yet, as we saw in the first three chapters, given the limited resources available to most schools—combined with their organized anarchy and busy kitchen characteristics—that level of innovation is very difficult to implement and institutionalize.

While schools, most of the time, need to effect more ambitious change, we need to acknowledge the value of small-scale innovation. For many organizations that is the more realistic route to improvement—perhaps the only route at a certain moment in their development. It appears to be the primary way in which the good schools discussed earlier got to be good.

We need to know more about how good schools become adaptable. In 1981, Miles called for ". . . more contingent analyses, showing, for example, under what contextual conditions active teacher involvement in planning change will be productive" (p. 111). David, who synthesized the literature on site-based management, concluded that there is a dearth of knowledge about the dynamics of local school decision making and change (1989, pp. 45-53). Finally, Clune and White concluded, after a review of thirty site-based management projects, that one important area for further research is to ''unravel issues'' relating to teacher participation in decision making, educator roles, and patterns of communication and interaction (1988, p. 31).

To contribute toward this unraveling, I conducted field studies of processes of curricular and instructional innovation over a five-year period in two Vermont high schools, Bromley and Mansfield (pseudonyms). The schools were selected from a pool of six medium-sized high schools (by Vermont standards) judged by a selection panel to be '' good'' high schools, but not ones known for being innovative. Five years was the boundary for the analysis so that two major imposed innovations, State Board of Education Basic Competency Regulations and the Public Law 94-142 staffing procedure, would be included.

I spent five weeks, full-time, in each school interviewing, distributing questionnaires, reading documents, and observing informally. I lived in each community during that period. Initial interviews (an average of 100 minutes each) were conducted with every administrator, counselor, special educator, and teacher. Thus the findings are based on the total relevant school populations. No attempt was made to assess whether one organization was ''better'' than the other. (See Appendix A for a description of the research methodology.)

In Vermont, as is the case throughout New England (with the exception of larger cities), schools have traditionally had decision-making autonomy in budgeting, curriculum, and staffing, the three basic decision areas associated with decentralization or site management (David, 1988, pp. 4-5). Based on my experiences working with administrators and teachers from other parts of the country, this kind of building-level control is not unusual, despite some of the current literature which implies that most schools are directed mainly by centralized district operations.

## THE SCHOOLS

Bromley, a 9-12 school in central Vermont built in 1958, had 500 students, a dropout rate of 4.5 percent, and 38 percent of its graduates going on to some form of higher education. The principal had been in his job for six years and had a full-time assistant. The average experience for the thirty-six teachers was eleven years. Twelve staff had bachelor's degrees and twenty-four had master's degrees. Bromley was unionized.

Five elementary schools representing rural populations of 8,349 people were "feeder" schools for the high school. One-third of the population was employed in agricultural or forest-related industries and about one-quarter in manufacturing. Average per capita income was about half that of national per capita income. Close to half the population had a high school education and close to 15 percent of families were classed as being below the poverty line. Despite these financial constraints, per-pupil costs were slightly above the state average for schools the size of Bromley.

Mansfield, a 7-12 school in northern Vermont built in 1970, had 400 students, a dropout rate of 3.0 percent, and 36 percent of its graduates going on to some form of higher education. The principal had been in his job for seven years and had a half-time assistant. The average experience for the thirty-one teachers was ten years. Eighteen staff had bachelor's degrees and thirteen had master's degrees. Mansfield was unionized. (Two years after my study, Mansfield became the first high school in Vermont to be selected as a "successful organization" under the U.S. Department of Education's Recognition Program.)

Three elementary schools representing rural populations of 3,863 people were "feeder" schools for the high school. About one-quarter of the population was employed in agricultural or forestry-related industries and about one-fifth in manufacturing. Average per capita income was about half that of the average national per capita income. Close to half the population had a high school education and close to 15 percent of families were classed as living below the poverty line. Despite these financial constraints, per-pupil costs were just slightly below the state average for schools the size of Mansfield.

Each principal was delegated authority by the superintendent over building maintenance, budget construction and management, curriculum development and management, hiring (subject to board approval), supervision, staff evaluation and development, and construction of board agendas in cooperation with the board chair. These are all characteristics of a site-managed school. The buildings were clean and well-maintained. Graffiti was rare. Vandalism costs were less than $400 a year.

The superintendents had business managers, but no assistants, and were responsible for the oversight of several elementary schools. Therefore, the site-managed high schools relieved them of another direct major supervisory task.

A comment by the Mansfield principal captures the philosophy of the principals relative to their building role.

> I'm the least important person here. I can be away all day and this place will still run. I'm really trying to decentralize control. I can't control everything anyway.

This philosophy led, in turn, to the principals delegating considerable decision-making responsibility to teachers in matters relating to curriculum and instruction.

## THE CONCEPTUAL FRAMEWORK

There are two major characteristics of this study that make it different from other studies about change. First, Bromley and Mansfield were selected on the basis of being "good" — not on the basis of being innovative. Other investigations (such as those described in Chapter 2) start by identifying schools that had adopted or developed an innovation, and then proceed to examine the dynamics of its implementation. The organizations were seen as innovative initially.

The second characteristic different about this research is its construction around the change model that emerged out of the Rand studies of "Federal Programs Supporting Educational Change" (Berman and McLaughlin, 1978, pp. 13-21; Berman in Lehming and Kane, 1981, pp. 264-274). That model (Figure 4.1) emphasized that change does not move in a linear fashion from one discrete stage to another; rather it is a highly complex, interactive process encompassing three phases: mobilization (sometimes referred to by other authors as adoption or initiation), implementation, and institutionalization. All three phases are usually occurring at different times and with different people. Even when something is institutionalized, conditions may lead to new thinking (mobilization) that, in turn, creates modifications in it. This was the case with the findings to be reported here. Change is not a stop and start act; in an adaptable school, change is recursive.

## ELEMENTS OF SMALL-SCALE CHANGE

> Most change in organizations results neither from extraordinary organizational processes or skill, but from relatively stable, routine processes that relate organizations to their environments. [March, 1981, p. 564]

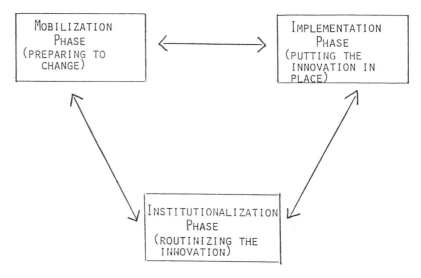

**Figure 4.1** Three Phases of Change.

How does change begin? What stimulates it? What motivates people to change? The instrumental elements include: types of innovations, teacher roles, stimuli for and sources of innovation, motivation to change, and leadership. In describing them, the recursive nature of the phases of the Rand Model is very much in evidence.

## Types of Innovations

To begin the research it was first necessary to identify the innovations that existed in the schools. Two forms emerged — policy and voluntary.

The policy changes were Basic Competency Regulations and Public Law 94-142 staffings, both of which were present in all high schools in the state. These will be discussed in Chapter 5. The rest of this chapter focuses on the voluntary types listed in Table 4.1.

### Observations about the Innovations

In a frequently cited study of change in district high schools in Illinois, Daft and Becker point out that ''. . . a good typology of innovations can enhance our understanding of the processes underlying innovation'' (1978, p. 139). Although recent studies (e.g., of the National Diffusion

TABLE 4.1 A Typology of Voluntary Innovations.

| | | Bromley | Mansfield |
|---|---|---|---|
| Course | A body of organized knowledge taught on a semester or year basis (e.g., Vermont Ecology, Data Processing) | n = 14 | n = 14 |
| Unit | A segment of a course (e.g., 4 weeks on mfg. in metals, 2 weeks on map skills in geography) | n = 8 | n = 9 |
| Theme | A topic of discourse or discussion (e.g., consumerism in home econ., sex equity in U.S. History) | n = 7 | n = 8 |
| Methods and Materials | Means of instruction and the implements for its delivery (e.g., games and simulations in French, new text in Basic English) | n = 5 | n = 3 |
| Technology | A technological device for aiding the learning process (e.g., microcomputer in math, memory typewriter in business education) | n = 2 | n = 4 |
| Structure | Work patterns or working relationships of organization members (e.g., double period for transcription, open classroom area for math) | n = 3 | n = 3 |
| TOTAL | | 39 | 41 |

Network) identify types of innovations, they do not place them into a workable typology nor do they examine the factors that may affect their implementation.

For veteran educators, there are no surprises in Table 4.1. All schools implement innovations like these, and good schools are particularly adept at installing new courses. But what is interesting is the variety of ordinary, small-scale types. In most cases, individual teachers initiated them, taught them, and were thus most affected by them. However, other innovations affected entire departments—such as several new courses (initiated by the principals) in social studies, English, and science that constituted an "innovation bundle" (Hall and Hord, 1987, p. 135). Another project that had some twenty urban, suburban, and rural high schools as its data base, also found that the organizations had implemented, over two years, numerous small-scale innovations (Rutherford and Austin, 1984, pp. 58-62).

Many people would class these kinds of changes as inherently simple—even insignificant—because, as Fullan contends, significant change is usually multidimensional in terms of materials or technology, approaches or methods, and alteration of beliefs (1982, pp. 30-35). While these Bromley and Mansfield innovations appear commonplace against these criteria, for the innovating teachers, tackling the theme of sex equity in social studies, the origins of life in biology, or a death and dying unit in English was complex, multidimensional, and demanding work.

Since they were site-managed, the only time Bromley and Mansfield required consistent principal, superintendent, and board involvement with voluntary innovations occurred when courses had to be approved. Then, budget implications, statutory responsibilities, and administrator philosophy brought the boards into the process because, in the words of the Bromley principal:

> It's essential that the board knows what's going on around here in curriculum. The administration has a responsibility to educate the board so it can make intelligent decisions.

The board chair, in turn, expressed mutual respect and an endorsement of site management:

> The board is here to deal with policy and finances. We hire administrators to think and get for us the best school we can have. The staff is to teach, work with the administrators, and do the best job it can for the youngsters.

The principals had considerable latitude about when they needed to involve the superintendent and board in decision making relative to innovations. While involvement always came when a change carried dollar signs (e.g., the purchase of computers or the acceptance of a new program), there was no hierarchical lid on innovations at Bromley and Mansfield—as evidenced by the fact that each school had a family living course that dealt with sex education, often a red flag in many communities.

Note that the data in Table 4.1 are purely quantitative. This study did not include an "impact assessment" of the innovation on the organization. (Just how does a unit, for example, measure up against an open classroom area for mathematics in terms of its effect on students and educators?)

Consider also the number of innovations. How many should high schools like these in these settings have implemented over a five-year period? How does one establish an "innovation baseline" against which to examine innovativeness? Is it even possible to do so when local contexts differ and each organization is affected differently by osmotic phenomena?

Finally, how accurate is the tally? The principals contended that if one included in the list changes in teaching styles, approaches to discipline, and alterations in professional attitudes and educational beliefs, there would be far more than eighty. I agree with them.

An interesting example of this "unknown factor" is when the principals talked about their need to consider changing the daily schedule. In each case there were too many study halls and not enough elective courses. The teachers concurred, and the Mansfield principal concluded, "I can manage the curriculum by building the schedule. And the schedule gives the gestalt of the program."

On one level, the schedule change was a large-scale innovation, but it also had an impact on student attitudes (more attention to studying), teacher attitudes (study halls were "no fun" to monitor and teachers felt relieved of a real burden), and curriculum, in that more courses could be offered to meet student needs (thus expanding options in "the shopping mall"). Educators recognize that schedule making of this kind can lead to "innovation bundles." For the critic who wants to see radical change, the schedule will not pass muster—it appears to be merely a routine management task. Yet developing different schedules was a key goal of the NASSP Model Schools Project discussed in Chapter 2, and it is today for Sizer's Coalition of Essential Schools (*Horace*, May 1989).

## Innovations and Attributes

The next step in the research was to place this topology of innovations in a grid against innovation attributes from the literature.

Rogers, one of the most noted students of innovation, states that change agents hoping to gauge potential reactions to certain innovations would find it helpful if they could know beforehand the critical attributes of innovations. He points out that the literature concentrates on the differences between people who might adopt an innovation and gives scant attention to differences between innovations (1983, pp. 210-211). Also, Daft and Becker conclude that it is much more useful to examine the attributes of innovations rather than thinking of them as a homogeneous category (pp. 120-127).

Table 4.2 represents an analysis of specific innovations at Bromley and Mansfield against six attributes drawn from Rogers (pp. 210-232) and Zaltman, Duncan, and Holbek (1973, pp. 33-50). The attributes include the four main characteristics of a change that Fullan (1982, pp. 57-63) found necessary for successful implementation—need, clarity, degree of complexity, and quality and practicality. The "high," "medium," and "low" assessments in Table 4.2 are qualitative, but they represent an example of the kind of analysis called for by researchers. This is not to say that in the organized anarchy and busy kitchen environments of Bromley and Mansfield, all innovations were passed through an innovation attribute screen before someone decided to mobilize for change. But it appears that the educators in these schools did that very thing intuitively.

Change agents can purposefully use this attribute screen when considering certain innovations. For example, when schools enter the computer field, they may view the computer as just another technology to be "installed." In reality, though, it creates numerous demands on the organization due to its inherent complexity and numerous implementation requirements. "Screening" the technology with the attributes could insure a better planned change. It might help avoid the situation faced by some schools where the lack of such planning has led to locked up banks of computers sitting idle for part of the day because provisions for adequate supervision and staff training were not considered before purchase. "Hidden" requirements such as these must be uncovered by proper screening in order to insure the successful implementation and institutionalization of innovations.

## Teacher Roles

Historically, teachers have enjoyed considerable autonomy in decision making within the classroom. A theme common to all the reports and studies of the 1980s is that "teachers should be provided with the discretion and autonomy that are the hallmarks of professional work" (Carnegie Forum on Education and the Economy, 1986, p. 56). Research tells us that effective employees in organizations like schools—which serve a reluctant, often unmotivated clientele—need considerable discretion to act (Katz and Kahn, 1978, p. 159).

To assess the presence of autonomy and job discretion at Bromley and Mansfield, each teacher completed a twenty-four item "Sense of

TABLE 4.2 Innovations and Attributes.

| | Relative Advantage (degree perceived as better than alternatives) | Compatibility (degree perceived as consistent with existing values and norms) | Complexity (degree perceived as difficult to understand and use) | Implementation Requirements (items and arrangements necessary to implement) | Trialability (degree of experimentation possible on limited basis) | Observability (degree to which innovation results are visible to others) |
|---|---|---|---|---|---|---|
| Course (e.g., Vt. Ecology) | hi | hi | medium | medium | medium | medium |
| Unit (e.g., Map Skills) | hi | hi | lo | lo | hi | medium |
| Theme (e.g., Consumerism) | hi | hi | lo | lo | hi | lo |
| Methods and Materials (e.g., Games and Texts) | hi | hi | lo | lo | medium | medium |
| Technology (e.g., Microcomputer) | hi | hi | hi | hi | medium | hi |
| Structure (e.g., Open area for Math) | medium | lo | hi | hi | lo | hi |

Autonomy Questionnaire'' scored on a 1 (low) to 6 (high) scale (Packard et al., 1976, pp. 211-251). The mean score for the respective staffs was 4.5 and 4.6. These outcomes are congruent with a national survey of staff-reported involvement in school decision making, where Vermont teachers ranked highest in choosing textbooks and instructional materials (93 percent) and in shaping the curriculum (85 percent) (Carnegie Foundation for the Advancement of Teaching, 1988, pp. 4-5).

## Stimuli for Innovation

Teachers were asked, ''What was the stimulus for the innovation you've described?'' Table 4.3 depicts the responses.

### *Observations about Stimuli for Change*

There was no pattern to the connection of certain stimuli with certain types of innovations. This conclusion—plus the fact that there was such a variety of stimuli—is similar to the findings of Huberman and Miles, who uncovered a host of what they called ''reasons/motives'' for adopting a National Diffusion Network or Title IV-C innovation (1984, pp. 44-52). Different, however, is the fact that administrative pressure on staff forced the adoption of most of those innovations. That factor contrasts with Table 4.3, which is dominated by teacher initiatives for small-scale innovations.

These stimuli have a distinct ''inner directedness'' (e.g., from teachers, students, principals). The schools were not subject to much direct environmental pressure to change.

Many of the innovations at Bromley and Mansfield were aimed at the vocation-bound student. This outcome contrasts with Daft and Becker's study, which found that teachers were inventive primarily concerning changes relative to the college-oriented curriculum, but needed to be prodded by administrators when it came to changes concerning the vocational-oriented program. In that case, local values focused on higher education.

At Bromley and Mansfield, local values did not favor the college-bound over the vocation-bound student (less than 40 percent of the graduating classes went on to higher education). Hence teachers, who

TABLE 4.3 Stimuli for Change.

| | |
|---|---:|
| Student interest or dissatisfaction (e.g., students not electing elective courses, failing grades, or "acting up" out of boredom) | 21 |
| Teacher ego, interest, or experience (e.g., the poor image of a course, special affinity for a pet subject, new information from a graduate course) | 13 |
| Laws, regulations, and accreditation visits (e.g., Title IX, PL 94-142, accreditation team suggesting a new course) | 10 |
| Teacher observation (e.g., students needing first-aid instruction for farm work, students needing sex education information not available through a community agency) | 7 |
| Teacher dissatisfaction (e.g., "I had to do something with this material. It was driving me crazy.") | 6 |
| Journals and newsletters (e.g., a death and dying unit from the English Journal) | 5 |
| Administrative direction (This category, although low in number, is not an accurate portrait of the principals' roles. It encompasses several changes through principal direction such as a "bundle" of course innovations in a department.) | 4 |
| School structure (e.g., a new study hall structure that affected "time on task," an open area that facilitated teaming in math) | 4 |
| Budget (addition or cuts) (e.g., a model office from state and federal vocational eduational assistance, creating a new course out of two courses due to RIFing)* | 3 |
| Culture change (e.g., carry over activities in physical education to meet leisure time needs) | 3 |
| The local public (e.g., parental complaints about numbers of failures in a government course) | 3 |
| Peers (e.g., suggesting the local paper as an outlet for work of a journalism class) | 1 |
| TOTAL | 80 |

*Reduction in Force.

felt the press of needs from a significant number of non-college-bound youngsters, responded to them with various innovations. In numerous instances, the principals made innovation interventions on behalf of all groups of students. Clearly, educators must attend to the range of local values as stimuli for change and not neglect some students in the process.

Although Bromley and Mansfield had a written philosophy and goals, they were not mentioned as a stimulus. This is not an uncommon research finding. For example, Boyer, in his noted analysis of the high school, found:

> When we asked teachers, principals, and students about school goals, their response frequently was one of uncertainty, amusement, or surprise. "What do you mean?" "Goals for what?" Some teachers just smiled. Others apologized for not knowing. [1983, p. 61]

However, no one (at Bromley and Mansfield) perceived the innovations as a bad fit with what the school was all about. There was an implicit "philosophical glue" bonding them. Innovation decision makers saw a positive relationship between changes and organization purposes and made rational choices—a finding similar to one in Daft and Becker's study (p. 129). In an organized anarchy, the connection between individual and organizational goals may be quite loose (March and Olsen, 1979, p. 16). Therefore, schools need to make more than a routine effort to connect them.

According to much of the literature, change should follow the classic pattern of problem-search-solution. However, at Bromley and at Mansfield, the usual initial stimulus for small-scale change did not grow formally out of a rationally defined problem, but emerged instead from educators' intuition, hypothesizing, and experience—modalities that some authors advocate as important ways to stimulate organizational improvement (March and Olsen, 1979, pp. 78-79). Other literature demonstrates that such mobilizing phenomena are not unique to these schools (Huberman and Miles, 1984, pp. 44-52; Daft and Becker, 1978, pp. 127-136; Louis and Miles, 1990). They also exist in well-run businesses (e.g., Kanter, 1983, pp. 129-205).

### Sources of Ideas

At Bromley and Mansfield teachers were asked, "Where did you get the idea to respond to the stimulus?" Twenty-one teachers named professional journals and newsletters, thirteen named discussions with peers, and twelve named college courses. Other responses were scattered among areas such as conferences, television, the school librarian, the principal, and textbooks.

Reading, talking, listening: these are the pivotal behaviors for acquiring ideas to respond to a change stimulus. The schools subscribed to journals, as did many staff, and the schools supported teachers financially when they enrolled in college courses. These information sources had considerable payoff, and demonstrate how central knowledge is to change. As is true for most schools, however, there was little money budgeted at Bromley and Mansfield to enable staff to attend conferences, places where professionals routinely obtain considerable information.

In keeping with the non-linear nature of change discussed thus far, it should be pointed out that in several instances the source of the idea for the innovation "arrived" in someone's mind before a stimulus or need was apparent.

For example, a Mansfield teacher attended a university course on writing and subsequently searched the curriculum for a place where the teaching of writing needed improvement. The result was an elective writing course. At Bromley, a teacher attended a course in vocational-technical education that led to the development of a new unit on metals for an industrial arts course.

The professional desire to be "enlightened" was a major factor in this process. As one teacher put it, "Most schools don't identify the problem. They come up with solutions first."

Sieber, in a major analysis of key incentives that encourage teacher innovation, points out that enlightenment has been undervalued, noting that, "There are reasons to believe that more up-to-date, informed, 'tuned-in' individuals take more initiative in educational change" (1981, p. 148). Such individuals search for solutions before there is an identified problem so that when one arises they are well-armed to respond.

Despite the importance of information in this process of improvement, it is interesting to note that no one in either school mentioned the ERIC system, the National Diffusion Network, or the State Department of Education as a source of ideas.

## Motivation to Change

At Bromley and Mansfield, autonomous teachers were stimulated to change by a variety of factors in the work environment. Why? Consider their responses to interview questions (drawn from Lortie's classic study of the teaching profession [1975, pp. 248-254]) related to motivation.

When asked, "What are the most important tasks you have to do as a teacher?" forty-seven out of fifty-nine responses dealt with role modeling, meeting the needs of students, and planning and organizing the day. Only four respondents mentioned ''developing and updating curriculum.''

When asked, ''What are the greatest satisfactions you get from teaching?'' eighty-one of 111 responses had to do with seeing students do well in school, working with them, and having control over the logistics of the day and the way work was done. Finally when asked, ''If you were given a gift of ten extra hours a week for work (and you were paid for it), how would you spend the time?'' Answers ranged (Bromley to Mansfield) from 25 percent to 18 percent on class preparation, 22 percent to 10 percent on curriculum development, 12 percent to 28 percent on counseling students, 16 percent to 13 percent on advising school activities, and 10 percent to 20 percent on more teaching. The responses are highly similar to what teachers told Lortie in 1963 (p. 163) and what they told follow-up researchers twenty years later (Kottcamp, Provenza, and Cohn, 1986).

For these teachers, the prime motivators to innovate were rooted in a variety of psychological factors. While there are other types of rewards that teachers can earn — extrinsic (money, prestige, power) and ancillary (work schedules, job security, time off) (Lortie, pp. 101-106) — both types do not fluctuate very much and cannot be manipulated directly by teachers. Psychic rewards, on the other hand, are within easy reach of teachers, if the workplace climate permits them to be obtained by the staff.

As the answers to the Bromley and Mansfield questionnaire demonstrate, teachers do not get ''kicks'' from dealing with discipline problems or building management. In schools where teachers have to spend inordinate time on issues like these, creative energy is diffused, rather than focused on tasks relating to instruction and learning that can affect psychological rewards. Getting these rewards is an incentive; it may be more important to stimulating innovation than first responding to a need. One teacher summed it nicely, ''I love to work with kids when I see them learn.''

In good schools, teachers feel focused on curriculum and instruction and their sense of efficacy is enhanced. Efficacy is being seen increasingly as a key variable in the school improvement process, because feeling that one can have a positive impact on one's immediate situation boosts energy and persistence in the face of challenges (Ashton and Webb, 1986, p. 3). In turn, one gains power in the workplace, and teacher empowerment is another theme running in current reports and studies (e.g., Carnegie Forum, *A Nation Prepared*; Maeroff, 1988). Finally, as Rogers contends, "Individual innovativeness is affected both by the individual's characteristics, and by the nature of the social system in which the individual is a member" (1983, p. 260).

Empowerment and thus innovativeness are aided by employees being successful at "small wins" — concrete, complete outcomes of a moderate scale that are in use. Small wins are motivational in that they enable people to respond to problem stimuli by doing something rather than being frustrated by inaction. Acting with success is rewarding. Continued frustration leads to feeling of powerlessness rather than empowerment (Weick, 1984, pp. 40-48). Continued frustration creates morale problems. Teachers at Bromley and Mansfield, as the data show, drew on small wins to respond to the various needs they encountered. Morale was positive in both organizations.

Schools have undervalued the impact that organizational climate and its accompanying forces can have on staff motivation. As was the case with Bromley and Mansfield, a vast reservoir of teacher talent, creativity, and drive is present in most schools, and it costs little to release it. But this reality tends to be overlooked in favor of a continued reliance on extrinsic approaches to motivation. This tendency is illustrated by a publication on teacher incentives — developed under the auspices of the three national administrator organizations — where there is no discussion about psychic rewards, but rather an extensive treatment of topics like compensation plans, career options, and enhanced professional responsibilities (Cresap, McCormick, and Paget, 1984).

Figure 4.2 depicts the variety of stimuli for decision making and innovation uncovered from the Bromley and Mansfield staffs.

## Leadership

At the time of the study, the Bromley principal had been in his job for six years and the Mansfield principal for seven. Both were active and assertive individuals who practiced "management by walking around"; were highly involved with staff, students, the board, and the community; and were concerned about and engaged in matters of curriculum and instruction. However, the latter happened around the cracks and edges of the job because their workpace was similar to the national research findings about the position discussed in Chapter 3.

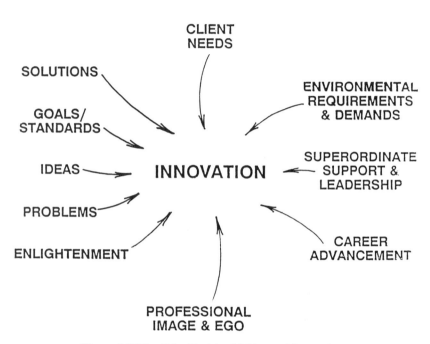

**Figure 4.2** Stimuli for Decision Making and Innovation.

The Bromley principal saw his role this way:

I plant the seed, leave it there, and water it from time to time. When it takes place you give away the ownership of it. The only people who may be aware of the change may be those involved in the transaction.

The Mansfield principal noted:

The focus here is on change as a process and not an event. People have to come to feel that an idea is theirs before they'll move. Things happen subtly, in low key ways.

The following comments by faculty members represent how most felt about their principals:

(Bromley)
He's very responsive and accommodating. He understands curriculum and knows the details of what's going on around here.

I'm very dependent on him being willing to support an idea and advocate for it. Without that backing after awhile you just give up.

(Mansfield)
He's on top of the latest trends. He seems to read all the magazines. He challenges us to think about what we're doing. If we as a department don't buy it, though, he doesn't force it on us.

He's continually trying to upgrade curriculum. I have the feeling that he's never quite satisfied with what's going on. He wants excellence.

These men were a mix of the initiator, manager, and responder styles of change facilitation identified by Hall and Hord (1987, pp. 215-257). A change facilitator is an administrator who sees him/herself as more of a colleague than a boss, and hence supports and assists teachers in their work. Each was far more an initiator and manager than a reactor to events. They engaged in countless interventions with their staffs—actions or events that influenced the use of an innovation (p. 143). Intervention incidents (the smallest level) included casual, isolated conversations in the hallways or over the lunchroom table; leaving an article in a mailbox; or repeated assistance to a teacher who was implementing an innovation. These patterns of behavior for the Bromley and Mansfield principals are in line with the Hall and Hord finding that responder administrators make far fewer interventions (p. 244).

By themselves, most interventions of this sort are rarely noticed. But through them the principals were able to nudge many small-scale changes so that bringing them about had become part of the normative climate of the organization. As a result, these successes with an innovation provided incentives that boosted efficacy and empowered staff. Corbett (1982), in a study of effective principal behavior relative to classroom change, and McAvoy (1987), in a study of effective principal behavior relative to staff development, found that commonplace intrinsic incentives provided by administrators — such as talking to teachers about their needs or inquiring how an innovation was progressing — had great impact on teacher attitudes and motivation. "Everyday acts" were important to new practices becoming part of the curriculum.

In addition to their change facilitator styles, the principals were also leaders in terms of what the literature tells us about that important organizational process (e.g., Hersey and Blanchard, 1988). They had the ability to respond to people with behaviors appropriate to the situation. Each was able to be directive or task-oriented as well as relationship-focused. For example, the Mansfield principal said,

> With most faculty they are basically on their own. They are in charge. However, there are a few that I've got on a shorter rein—they have less freedom now.

This is not to say that they were models of administrative behavior. At times the Bromley principal was seen as not directive enough regarding needed curricular and instructional improvements, as not intervening with a teacher when he should have, and as placing too much emphasis on relationships. At times the Mansfield principal was seen as too task-focused and somewhat overbearing. But, in sum, these men were seen very positively by their staffs, the students, the board, and the community. They were the instructional leaders of their schools, and demonstrated what research points to as the critical element of leadership accomplishment — positive leader-member relationships. "The *most important* single element in situational control is the amount of loyalty, dependability, and support you, as the leader, get from those with whom you work" (Fiedler and Chemers, 1984, p. 47).

This chapter has described the elements of small-scale innovation as revealed through an examination of improvement processes in the Bromley and Mansfield high schools. Chapter 5 will outline a "marketplace model of change" constructed around the types of innovations, teacher roles, stimuli for innovation, sources of ideas, motivation to change, and leadership.

# Good Schools and Small-Scale Change

> An organization is a collection of choices looking for problems, issues and feelings looking for decision situations in which they might be aired, solutions looking for issues to which they might be the answer, and decision makers looking for work. [Cohen, March, and Olsen, 1972, p. 2]

If decision makers were to follow conventional wisdom, they would take only those actions suggested by the goals of the organization. After all, should not thinking precede action and action relate to the societal mission of the organization in the first place? This conception of decision making is deeply imbedded in our culture. Underlying it is the Deweyian model of felt difficulty, problem analysis, search for solutions, consideration of alternatives, and choosing. Within this framework, impulse, intuition, faith, and tradition are not given much credence; they are outside of the mainstream of what is most trusted as the basis for choosing and changing. (These ideas and many that follow in this chapter, are drawn primarily from March, 1981; March, 1983; and March and Olsen, 1979 and 1986.)

Planning is stressed and orderly change is highlighted. Many good books on the subject stock library shelves. Because we ''ought'' to do things according to this model, we try to act that way in schools because it is widely accepted, logical, and sensible. Politically, it becomes difficult to espouse a radically contrasting approach. ''The appearance of rational action legitimates the organization in the environment it faces, deflects criticism, and ensures a steady flow of resources into the organization'' (Weick in Lincoln, 1985, p. 110).

Sometimes we are successful in following convention, but, as the literature review demonstrated in Chapter 2, the conventional approach does not have a starry history within the organized anarchy and busy kitchen features of educational organizations. This approach, given the hectic and fragmented pace of work, demands too much time and information from decision makers, and assumes that most of them share the same goals. Often the "round" theory does not fit with the reality of the "flat" experiences (or vice versa) thus creating frustration and sometimes disenchantment with how it ought to work (March, 1983, pp. 32-35). Employees begin to doubt their abilities and become frustrated when they try to influence organizational events.

Fortunately, we have begun to see things differently. Our expanding cultural perspective liberates us from focusing narrowly on how organizations "should" behave. "Rational decision-making processes can be observed in schools; so can accidents" (Clark and McKibbin, 1982, p. 671). Our broader vision allows us to view the "accidents" as more than anomalies. For while the traditional perspective is deeply imbedded in our collective psyches and in our political and social institutions, the new perspective allows us to see another path through the maze. This path — "humble decision making" in the words of Etzioni (1989) — stresses adaptation through broad scans of issues and choices combined with detailed examination of localized facts and alternatives. Flexibility, caution, and the capacity to move ahead with partial knowledge are characteristics of this less than heroic and dramatic approach to changing organizations.

In this chapter we shall fit together the findings from Chapter 4 into a "marketplace model of change" that draws on some of this new literature to provide insights and ideas about an alternative route to school improvement. The term *model* should not be seen as another purely rationalistic conception of organizational change and innovation. Rather it incorporates the affective and cognitive elements identified at Bromley and Mansfield, with new concepts from the literature. The goal: a route through the maze, a working map of new understandings about educational change.

## THE MARKETPLACE AND MOBILIZATION

Some general outcomes from this part of the research are strikingly similar to findings from Daft and Becker's study of innovative high schools.

For example, they concluded that there was a disorganized nature to the processes, that innovation takes place in different areas within the organization, and that different innovations follow different routes to adoption. They also found high compatibility between their findings and the ideas of the organized anarchy and garbage can decision processes (pp. 164-181). However, their survey project did not obtain qualitative data to explain the dynamics behind their observations.

The marketplace is an appropriate metaphor through which to explain the qualitative data, relative to mobilization, that emerged from Bromley and Mansfield. These phenomena connect strongly to those uncovered by research into other good schools and they are also similar to the innovation processes found in excellent businesses. In those situations, supportive work climates provided rewards to relatively autonomous individuals or groups who invented new products or practices that led to improved organizational performance. "Innovating companies provide the freedom to act, which arouses the desire to act" (Kanter, 1983, p. 142). Many creative activities were undertaken without planned precision.

In a marketplace, behavior generally is rooted in incentives. The market structure provides boundaries within which individuals buy and sell. Booths, however, are loosely coupled to one another. Individuals are motivated by a variety of personally oriented incentives, but, other than selling within the framework of the market, there are few organization-level incentives that motivate. What tend to be more important to people are the satisfaction and rewards that come from working within the context of the marketplace environment and its overall mission. Intentionality undergirds action, but it is primarily the intentionality of individuals and not that of the market. There is rationality in the marketplace, but feelings, intuition, and values are powerful determinants of behavior (Clark and McKibbin, 1982, p. 671; Larson, 1991).

## GARBAGE CAN DECISION PROCESSES

Within the marketplace, organization-level decisions are made commonly through "choice opportunity situations," the occasions when the organization is expected to produce a decision. Situations are a "meeting place" for issues and feelings, solutions, and participants (Cohen, March, and Olsen, 1979, pp. 25-27). At the administrative level in schools, some typical choice situations are analyzing test results, budgeting, scheduling, assigning staff, conducting classroom evaluation visits, participating in staff development sessions, and attending meetings of all kinds. At the teacher level, some routine choice situations are lesson planning; course development and revision; and the construction, giving, and interpretation of tests.

The choice opportunity situations can be thought of as a garbage can, a collection device for the elements of problems/concerns; participant interests, competencies, attitudes, and values; and potential solutions to problems/concerns.

> The garbage can process . . . is one in which problems, solutions, and participants move from one choice opportunity to another in such a way that the nature of the choice, the time it takes, and the problems it solves all depend on a relatively complicated intermeshing of the mix of choices available at any one time, the mix of problems that have access to the organization, the mix of solutions looking for problems, and the outside demands on the decision makers. [Cohen, March, and Olsen, 1979, p. 36]

Figure 5.1 depicts the concept. The three elements mix—in ways not clearly observable—and the can (situation) gets full. The arrows should not be interpreted to indicate that the elements enter the can virtually simultaneously; usually they do not.

Eventually the can has to be emptied through a choice opportunity—a decision. That decision may be to change or not to change. Measured against the conventional, rational view of how organizations should function, this process seems vague—even irrational—but given that schools are not tight and tidy bureaucracies, the process is "normal" (Cohen, March, and Olsen, p. 37).

## THE MARKETPLACE MODEL

Figure 5.2, drawing on the garbage can motif and findings from Bromley and Mansfield, outlines how the contributing elements might look in more specific terms.

The element of problems/concerns (from Table 4.3) represents the stimuli that prodded teachers and administrators (participants) to begin thinking about the need to change. Then participant interests, competencies, attitudes, and values meshed with the types of voluntary innovations (Table 4.1) that became solutions.

These elements flow into the choice situations that exist within Sarason's programmatic and behavioral "regularities," which are present in all human situations. In schools, regularities include the

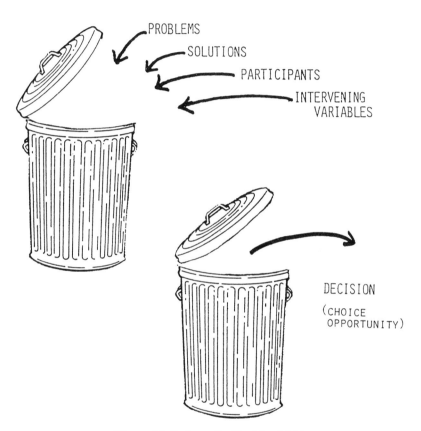

**Figure 5.1** Garbage Can Decision Making.

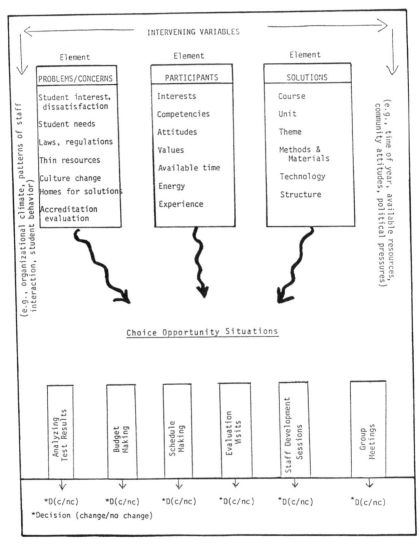

**Figure 5.2** A Marketplace Model of Change.

schedule, the size and composition of classes, the organization of curriculum, and patterns of instruction and student-teacher interaction (1982, pp. 95-117). These commonplace events, processes, and practices are powerful impediments to large-scale change or any type of restructuring; packed together they serve to reinforce the image that "the more things change the more they stay the same." Meanwhile, small-scale changes occur, often unnoticed by most observers.

Intervening variables in Figure 5.2 refer to organizational and environmental forces that affect when and how the elements enter the can and make decision making sometimes predictable and sometimes unpredictable. For example, in Vermont during the doldrums of "mud season" in March, few teachers are in a frame of mind to engage in creative school improvement activities. The appearance of an "anti-tax" community group at a town meeting could cause trouble for the most well-prepared budget. A controversial film by a teacher for use in a family living course could lead to school board interference in course content by a previously delegating board.

The particular choice situation may be a routine, institutionalized one (e.g., scheduling); it may be triggered by an external event from the environment (e.g., a special meeting to deal with a defeated budget); or it may be created to expressly improve the situation (e.g., a retreat to develop a school mission statement) (Christensen, 1979, pp. 373-377).

Innovations at Bromley and Mansfield were brought about largely through existing choice opportunity situations. Increasingly, research is pointing to their value and the value of "everyday acts" (as described in Chapter 3 relative to the principal's role) as key factors in school improvement. For example, a review of the literature on the instructional management role of the principal revealed that the following types of activities can have a great impact on school improvement: budgeting, scheduling, appointment of people to committees, public recognition of teachers for their achievements, strategic control of information about a new program, and lobbying for program support with senior administrators (Bossert et al., 1982, p. 51). These are some of the ordinary managerial activities that all principals must carry out if they are to administer a well-run organization. As another study put it,

They require no new program, no innovation, no extensive change. The success of these activities for instructional management hinges, instead, on the principal's capacity to connect them to the instructional system. [Dwyer et al., 1983, p. 54]

Making this connection is very dependent on conscious use of the choice situations for improvement rather than just routine purposes. Being more aware of when they occur, who is or could be involved, how often they occur, and their value/utility is a first step in this direction (Figure 5.3). For instance, rather than observing a teacher and then filling out a rating form and placing it in a mailbox without discussion, the effective principal uses the opportunity to also discuss curriculum and possible needs for change. Rather than placing standardized test results on her office shelf and not informing the staff of the outcomes, the effective principal develops a ''game plan'' of incidents (Hall and Hord, 1987, pp. 177-213) whereby the tests are fitted into the larger scheme of school improvement plans. The Bromley and Mansfield principals and teachers were adept at using the available choice situations to make their organizations better.

## HOW THE PROCESS WORKS

Here are some examples that show how the marketplace process of change worked in the schools.

### Bromley

a.   A social studies teacher with a strong psychology background was ''getting bored'' with his history courses, wanted to use his psychology training, and wanted to provide students with a course in adolescent psychology. As he put it, ''It was largely self-serving on my part.'' His department chair, department members, and the principal agreed that such a course was needed and that he should make a proposal to the board before late fall to make sure there were not any budget implications. Also, the course would need to be approved before late winter when the program of studies would be printed in anticipation of student scheduling in the spring.

The board turned down the initial proposal because of concerns about a unit on sexuality. However, the principal encouraged him to address the concerns and resubmit the proposal. He did and it was approved.

b.   Basic Competency Regulations of the State Board of Education (in reading, writing, speaking, listening, reasoning, and mathematics) presented Bromley with an opportunity to help students who had low

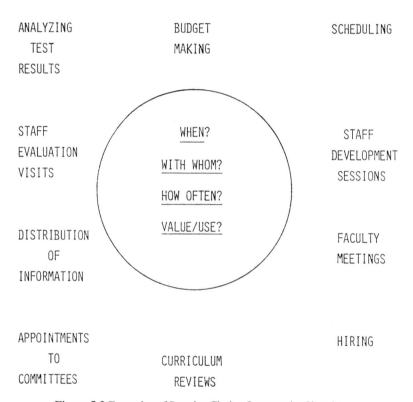

ANALYZING          BUDGET              SCHEDULING
   TEST            MAKING
RESULTS

STAFF             WHEN?                STAFF
EVALUATION                            DEVELOPMENT
VISITS            WITH WHOM?          SESSIONS

                  HOW OFTEN?

DISTRIBUTION      VALUE/USE?          FACULTY
   OF                                 MEETINGS
INFORMATION

APPOINTMENTS                          HIRING
    TO            CURRICULUM
COMMITTEES        REVIEWS

**Figure 5.3** Examples of Regular Choice Opportunity Situations.

literacy skills (a concern of teachers and the administration). At first, after the regulations were in effect and students had been tested, those needing additional help were aided by teachers in study halls. This arrangement was not satisfactory because staff had monitoring duties to perform and could not give the necessary attention to tutoring.

The chair of the English Department proposed to the principal the idea of a "Competency Class" that would be part of a teacher's load, and that during every study hall a teacher would be available to work with students on a "pull-out" basis. To make that teacher available, an aide would be hired for study hall supervision. The principal thought that it was a "super idea" and took it to the board because it had budget implications. It was approved for the next year. The principal also had to manipulate the schedule to accommodate the innovation.

c.    Part of the assignment for a new Home Economics teacher was a course in "Child Development." Within a year she found the content unexciting — "I couldn't stand the material any longer."

Students did not find it interesting either, as enrollments had been declining. As she put it, "Image was a big problem. Kids think of Home Ec as all cooking and sewing."

She talked with the principal about her concerns. They agreed that the course was important, particularly because there were so few opportunities in the immediate area for students to gain this formal knowledge out of school. He found money to support her taking a summer graduate course that would strengthen her background and perhaps spark ideas to change the situation. The next year she began to modify course content and methodology and gradually converted it into a laboratory. Students observed and worked with pre-school children who came to the school for the class. Parent relationships and general birth control information were added as units (being an existing course, the board was not asked to approve this additional content). The course became one of the most popular ones in the department.

## Mansfield

a.    A science teacher was assigned some mathematics courses as part of his schedule. Mathematics was not his first love and he did not feel that he was doing his best work in that subject. So he began to think about other possibilities in science that would address student needs. He talked with his chairman and the principal about his concerns and they decided to do a student survey regarding current and future science offerings.

The result was an experiment with a new forestry course for students who wanted to learn about managing a woodlot for home maintenance purposes (the school was in a rural area where knowledge about forest management for lay or career purposes was important) or for students in the vocation-oriented curriculum who might seek employment in a forestry-related field. A considerable amount of mathematics and engineering material was included in the content.

The course became one of the most popular courses in the school curriculum. In addition, a very successful outcome was the construction, by students, of a sugar house in the woods near the school. They produced and sold maple syrup, with profits going to the school for other projects.

b. An industrial arts teacher was confronted with the problem of how to attend to the needs of high-achieving students, who were so few in number at each grade level that the school could not offer them a course because of fiscal constraints. He could see that failure to respond to these students might adversely affect future enrollments in his elective program.

He proposed to the principal an independent study option as the solution as well as one that would aid the school's goal of doing more for gifted and talented youngsters. To implement it he would not supervise study halls, and extra assignments would be minimized. The proposal was accepted by the principal and the innovation has been an important part of the industrial arts program.

c. The principal, who met regularly with the business education department, reminded the staff that there were state and federal vocational education grants available for the purchase of equipment and materials. In his words, "Budgets are a planning tool. They force people to think about what they're doing. They should have a maintenance and a change function."

After one of these discussions, a teacher, influenced by some articles and her work on a state curriculum guide committee, realized that this might be a time to modernize the department's office equipment and also provide more "hands on" experiences for students through simulation materials. These ideas coincided with a grant proposal deadline. The application was approved and resulted in the acquisition of a word processing unit and a model office occupations room.

## Observations about Small-Scale Change

Small-scale innovation was driven primarily by the elements of the garbage can decision process rather than by the rational problem-solving approach. Although emotions and intuition played a major part in the process, teachers and administrators at Bromley and Mansfield were not irrational in their behavior. Their actions were intentional but intentionality was rarely attached consciously to organizational goals.

Schools, as we saw in Chapter 3, are laden with special characteristics that cause marketplace-driven behavior to be a potent spur for small-scale change. As Cohen, March, and Olsen observe,

> Measured against a conventional normative model of rational choice, the garbage can process does seem pathological, but such standards are not really appropriate since the process occurs precisely when the preconditions of more "rational" models are not met. [1979, p. 37]

At the same time, these characteristics constitute additional reasons why it is so difficult to "restructure" schools while at the same time quite possible, under the right conditions, to cause important improvements through less dramatic approaches.

Weick, who has studied extensively the processes of change in loosely coupled systems, concludes that in such systems innovation is continuous, small-scale, improvisational, accommodative, and local (in Goodman et al., 1982, p. 390). It represents "small wins" (to be discussed in Chapter 7).

As we saw in Chapter 3, a major force maintaining the basic regularities of schooling is the inherent instability of the classroom, which centers on a clientele that, to a large extent, would rather be somewhere else. However, this fact can also be the cause of innovation because good teachers continually modify what they do to keep attention and control, and to promote learning. Realizing that such adaptive behavior is vital to success, teachers work to add to their "recipes for busy kitchens" so they will be armed to meet a variety of unpredictable situations. At Bromley and Mansfield, the adopted or developed innovations were teacher vehicles for school improvement.

Information was a key factor in the success of teachers stockpiling tentative solutions to the problems they faced or anticipated facing. Information is instrumental to solution generation. As we have seen, reading professional literature, having discussions with peers, and attending college courses topped the list of ways in which the Bromley and Mansfield staffs garnered ideas for change.

Most teachers in these schools were similar to the "idea-champions" studied by Daft and Becker—those individuals who bring about a change. In such cases, their willingness to believe in an idea, to expend effort on implementation, to persist in carrying it over the inevitable rough spots, and to enlist the support and help of someone else were critical dimensions of successful innovation (1978, pp. 210-211).

Why do innovations fail? Fullan points out that those trying to get others to change too often ignore what a particular innovation *means* to those who actually would do the changing. How people experience change is their phenomenology, or their subjective reality (1982, p. 4). The teachers at Bromley and Mansfield had worked out their phenomenology for change through the steps they used in initiating small-scale innovations. They paid attention to their environments and responded with innovations that fit their organizational territory. The principals, because they were knowledgeable about that territory and their teachers as individuals, did not force innovations on them that were alien to that phenomenology.

As has been pointed out, the organizational climates of Bromley and Mansfield played a key role in the generation of the innovations discussed. The principals were pivotal in creating and sustaining that climate and, as was described in Chapter 4, they initiated and managed events, rather than merely reacting to them.

However, because so many innovations were initiated by teachers, at first glance these administrators might seem to be cast in roles of managers and reactors to change. Here it is appropriate to mention again that the most evident initiating behavior was connected to the "bundles" of innovations within a department that were portrayed in Chapter 4. Often the principals "got the ball rolling" but then left the main responsibility to the staffs to mobilize for and implement a change. Also, the initiating actions were often of the "incident" type, which were invisible to most observers.

Both men realized that ". . . much of the job of an administrator involves making the bureaucracy work" (March, 1983, p. 22). By making the schools work, they provided teachers an additional slice of time to initiate change and created and sustained a climate conducive to such action. The staffs did not have to be involved in the student control and building maintenance activities, which they did not see as part of their role.

All organizations compete for the attention and time of their employees, and schools, being organized anarchies as well as bureaucracies, have a particularly difficult task in this regard. Many internal and external forces tug at educators. Good schools find ways to husband the resources of attention and time so they are channeled more toward improvement than toward maintenance activities.

Data weigh heavily on the effective side of the scale for the principals of Bromley and Mansfield. However, they tended to rely on existing choice situations for school improvement efforts. They could have initiated more choice situations to try to alter teacher thinking about the need for more ambitious change (e.g., using an inservice day to examine societal trends and their possible impact on programs) and to implement innovations that would have had more organizational-level impact (the only larger-scale innovations that had been adopted or developed in each school within the five-year period of the study were imposed from outside).

This chapter has described the dynamics of small-scale innovation within the organized anarchy and busy kitchen environments of good schools, particularly as the dynamics relate to the mobilization phase of change. Chapter 6 will examine additional findings from Bromley and Mansfield that emerge from the phases of implementation and institutionalization. Underlying the findings is the interacting and recursive nature of the three phases.

# Magnifying the Innovation Map

Change will be most successful when its support is geared to the diagnosed needs of the individual users. If change is highly personal, then clearly different responses and interventions will be required for different individuals. Paying attention to each individual's progress can enhance the improvement process. [Hord et al., 1987, p. 6]

What happens to an innovation after it moves from the mobilization phase into implementation? Will it be used as intended by the adopters or developers? How do "users" react to the innovation, and how do those reactions affect its implementation? What factors determine whether the innovation will become a "permanent" part of organizational routines, become so modified that it is difficult to recognize it in its original form, or disappear with little or no trace?

In this chapter we will examine "up close" some voluntary innovations included in Chapters 4 and 5 and two policy innovations—placing them under a symbolic magnifying glass. The purpose is to gain additional understanding about the details of change, particularly at the level of the individual experiencing the change during the phases of implementation and institutionalization. These details will be amplified by drawing on the Levels of Use and Stages of Concern components of the Concerns-Based Adoption Model.

Upon completing this chapter, readers should develop further their "theory of changing" because this chapter contains additional concepts, technical information, and human relations knowledge that, as described in the Introduction, are the components of such a theory. They all can be joined with material contained in the Marketplace Model.

## IMPLEMENTATION

The literature reviewed in Chapter 2 revealed that since the 1970s, implementation has been studied more extensively than either mobilization or institutionalization. Adoption and development were the focus of research in the 1960s. The studies about implementation fall into two broad categories, fidelity and process (Fullan and Pompret, 1977, p. 340). *Fidelity* is the degree to which the use of the adopted innovation is "faithful" to the original design. Adoption is a sensible avenue to improvement because it shortcuts development time, utilizes (in most cases) an innovation that has been "debugged," to some degree, elsewhere, and usually saves money.

Because situations differ in terms of the organizational characteristics outlined in Chapter 3 and numerous "intervening variables" as discussed in the last chapter, many of these innovations have to be adapted, before or after implementation, to fit the local setting. However, excessive adaptation or neglect of a vital component of an innovation may lessen the impact the innovation was intended to have when adopted. Excessive adaptation may lead implementors to believe that they are really using a new practice and have changed how they do things when in fact they have not changed. This is the "false clarity" described by Fullan (1982, p. 28). In regard to neglect of a component, some schools have adopted mastery learning but have not supported the creation of correctives or enrichment activities that are integral to its integrity. Others have adopted the Madeline Hunter instructional skills program but have not trained teachers in vital components like establishing anticipatory set or guided practice.

The second category of implementation research examines the *process* of change—the dynamics of the interactive, developmental aspects of how implementation occurs. This chapter focuses on this line of inquiry.

### Examining the Process

I chose to examine change processes at Bromley and Mansfield through Concerns-Based Adoption Model (CBAM) instrumentation. This model (Figure 6.1) emerged from extensive research conducted for more than a decade by Hall and Hord and their colleagues on innovation in public schools and colleges (Hall and Hord, 1987; Hord et al., 1987). The instrumentation allows probing into change phenomena through questionnaires and interviews rather than relying on observation.

In the model, the *Resource System* represents the people, materials, money, and other resources available to the change activity. The *Change*

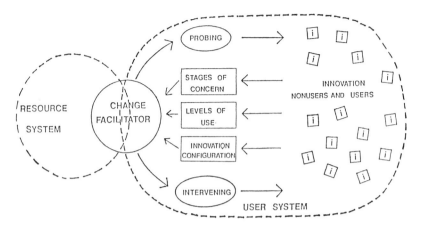

**Figure 6.1** The Concerns-Based Adoption Model. (Hord, et al. 1987, p. 10. Copyright, Southeast Educational Development Laboratory, 1987. Reprinted by permission.)

*Facilitator* is the person(s) responsible for giving leadership to the change effort. In schools this person might be the principal, a teacher, or a department head. *Stages of Concern* represent the affective side of change – the feelings, attitudes, and perceptions of the implementor and sometimes others involved with the innovation. *Levels of Use* represent the actual behaviors of the implementor. *Configurations* represent the forms that an innovation takes as it is used. Finally, *Interventions* represent the actions of the facilitator that influence the individual's use of the innovation.

Underlying the model are several assumptions (Hord et al., 1987, pp. 5-7):

(1) Change is a process, not an event.
(2) Change is accomplished by individuals.
(3) Change is a highly personal experience.
(4) Change involves developmental growth.
(5) Change is best understood in operational terms (what it will mean to the user; how practice will be affected).
(6) Change facilitators should focus on individuals, the innovation, and the context.

Drawing on this model, we will examine the Levels of Use and Stages of Concern at Bromley and Mansfield. In these schools, interventions were identified through the "everyday acts" and choice situations described in Chapters 4 and 5 relative to voluntary innovations. They also apply to two policy innovations, which were the only large-scale innovations found in the schools. The first policy innovation is the Vermont Basic Competency Regulations, mandated in 1977 by the State Board of Education and phased out as a regulation in 1991. It was phased out because the state determined that the competencies had now been infused into the regular curriculum. These regulations required schools to test the competency of all students in the areas of reading, writing, speaking, listening, mathematics, and reasoning. Beginning with the class of 1981, the successful mastery of competencies in these areas became a prerequisite for graduation. Prior to that date, it was left to each school to develop a system for implementing them—how to teach for mastery, how to monitor student progress, how to test, and how to keep records.

The second policy innovation is the staffings procedure required by Public Law 94-142, the Education for All Handicapped Children Act, which became law in 1975. Under this procedure each school has to hold periodic meetings of "basic staffing teams" (at minimum composed of the special education teacher in the school or district, the teacher of the child with a handicap, and one other staff member, usually a counselor or administrator) to assess the needs of children who appeared eligible for special education services and to recommend appropriate assistance. Eligibility resulted in the writing of an Individualized Educational Program (IEP). As with the Competencies, it was the school's responsibility to design its approach to implementation.

Both the competencies and the staffings were broadly defined rather than specifically delineated innovations. Neither of them met the four criteria that research demonstrates are associated with successful implementation: (1) the degree to which users see it as needed, (2) the clarity of the goals of the innovation and the means to implement them, (3) the complexity of the innovation or the degree to which it is difficult to implement, and (4) the degree to which the innovation is perceived to be of quality and practicality (Fullan, 1982, pp. 57-63). In other words, there was no true form of either innovation that the users had to implement (the fidelity concept) but there was considerable *process* involved if the Competencies and the Staffings were to be implemented with few hitches.

The principals assumed an active role in working with their staffs to implement these policies, but, as we shall see, each approached the task differently.

We will examine implementation of the voluntary and policy innovations through the Levels of Use and Stages of Concern methodology.

## Levels of Use

Levels of Use (LoU) is explored through an interview—a validated, focused methodology that enables a researcher to assess the behavior of individuals implementing an innovation (Loucks, Newlove, and Hall, 1975). Table 6.1 outlines these behaviors.

In the two schools, twenty-nine interviews were conducted at Bromley and twenty-four at Mansfield, each for an average of fifty minutes. The purpose was to examine how teachers were using the voluntary innovations (i.e., courses, units, themes, etc.) and the Competencies. No teacher declined to be in the LoU population. Staffings were not in-

TABLE 6.1 Levels of Use of the Innovation: Typical Behaviors.

| Levels of Use | Behavioral Indices of Level |
|---|---|
| 0  NONUSE | No action is being taken with respect to the innovation. |
| I  ORIENTATION | The user is seeking out information about the innovation. |
| II  PREPARATION | The user is preparing to use the innovation. |
| III  MECHANICAL USE | The user is using the innovation in a poorly coordinated manner and is making user-oriented changes. |
| IVA  ROUTINE | The user is making few or no changes and has an established pattern of use. |
| IVB  REFINEMENT | The user is making changes to increase outcomes. |
| V  INTEGRATION | The user is making deliberate efforts to coordinate with others in using the innovation. |
| VI  RENEWAL | The user is seeking more effective alternatives to the established use of the innovation. |

cluded, because these were not classroom-type innovations but rather a schoolwide process and practice.

## Observations from the LoU Interviews

The voluntary innovations had been in use for an average of two years, and the process to test for the Competencies had been worked on for three years. So it is interesting to note:

- With one exception, all teachers involved with the mandated innovation were at the IVA routine level (see Table 6.1). The one exception was at the LoU III mechanical level.
- On the other hand, eighteen users of voluntary innovations were at Level IVB, refinement—six at Bromley and twelve at Mansfield.

At the IVB level, the users try to increase the impact of the change on the client. They are not satisfied and they aim for improvement.

In the interviews, teachers at the refinement level were of the opinion that their innovation was having a considerable positive effect on student learning and attitudes, and that it had potential to have even more of an effect. Therefore, they believed it was well worth their time and effort to refine it. These staff members felt the sense of efficacy (discussed in earlier chapters) that research tells us is an important factor in successful implementation. The mandated innovations did not foster a similar reaction.

Being able to refine an innovation can be an important source of satisfaction and even revitalization to a teacher operating in a busy kitchen, where psychic rewards are so important to motivation. Empowerment is being generated. Staff at the refinement LoU are also at a readiness level in terms of ability and willingness to change (Hersey and Blanchard, 1988, pp. 183-186). Hence a supervisor would have considerable opportunity to affect teacher behavior even further in the direction of school improvement tasks.

## The Principal's Role

The factor that seems to explain the difference between the number of staff at the refinement level in one school compared to the other is the more initiating and interventionist behavior of the Mansfield principal in matters relating directly to curriculum and instruction. During the research, I observed each principal in numerous situations over a five-week period. A scan of incident interventions by them with their staffs (e.g., hallway conversations, leaving articles in mailboxes for teachers to read, following up on requests for assistance) gave a decided edge to the Mansfield principal in being more active.

However, the difference was not only in the sheer number of small-scale interventions. The Mansfield principal operated with *policy*, *game plan*, and even *strategy* type interventions in his repertoire (Hall and Hord, pp. 177-213).

(1) *Policies*, formal and informal, set parameters within which change can occur. For example, the process of budget building involved teachers systematically throughout the school year.

(2) A *game plan* is where a facilitator orchestrates incident interventions into a larger scheme to achieve a goal. At Mansfield, the principal's game plan involved distributing readings about new curriculum trends, staff evaluation sessions, parent and student feedback about the quality of a department's curriculum, and meetings with individual teachers and department members — all of which led to a decision to drop several elective courses and substitute several new courses (a "bundle of innovations") to replace them.

(3) *Strategy* interventions move beyond game plans into major actions that shift organizational direction. At Mansfield, calculated changes in departmental offerings over a period of years altered the complexion of that component of the school's program.

The Mansfield principal's favorite analogy for his role was that of an orchestra leader.

> The principal is the key to where the school is going. He is an orchestra leader, keeping the sections of the orchestra in balance. But he doesn't have to play every instrument. And its crucial for him to remember that a fifth grade orchestra is very different from a high school one.

This behavior is similar to the directive, task-focused behavior that Hersey and Blanchard (1988) and Glickman (1990) state is important for administrators to exhibit along with a range of other behaviors. This kind of behavior tells staff that what they are doing is important, that the administrator is interested in the activity and willing to put energy into supporting staff so that it will succeed, and that small wins are vital to organizational improvement.

As Hall and Hord assert (1987, p. 102), individuals at the LoU IVB refinement level make adaptations aimed at increasing the chances that the innovation will have positive outcomes. Sometimes the assistance of a facilitator can help someone move usage further along the LoU continuum. At Bromley and Mansfield, the principals assumed this role most of the time because department chairs had heavy teaching loads with the administrative part of their roles. (Their chair assignment was restricted largely to management tasks such as scheduling and ordering supplies. They had no delegated authority to discipline their staffs.)

### Stages of Concern (from interviews)

At the conclusion of the Levels of Use interviews, teachers were asked an open-ended question about the concerns they had about the use of the innovation—"When you think about __, what are you concerned about?"

TABLE 6.2 Stages of Concern: Typical Expressions
of Concern about the Innovation.

| Stages of Concern | | Expressions of Concern |
|---|---|---|
| I M P A C T | 6 REFOCUSING | I have some ideas about something that would work even better. |
| | 5 COLLABORATION | I am concerned about relating what I am doing with what other instructors are doing. |
| | 4 CONSEQUENCE | How is my use affecting kids? |
| T A S K | 3 MANAGEMENT | I seem to be spending all my time getting material ready. |
| S E L F | 2 PERSONAL | How will using it affect me? |
| | 1 INFORMATIONAL | I would like to know more about it. |
| | 0 AWARENESS | I am not concerned about it (the innovation). |

Hord, et al., 1987, p. 31, copyright, Southwest Educational Development Laboratory, 1987. Used by permission.

Stages of Concern (SoC) are depicted in Table 6.2.

## Observations about the SoC Interviews

The relatively veteran faculties (average experience at Bromley — eleven years; average at Mansfield — ten) did not have concerns about the innovations per se, but some had intense feelings about the management of the change — handling time, securing materials, etc.

Some Stage 3 concerns were

- A teacher responsible for implementing Basic Competencies said, ''All I seem to do is file stuff.''
- A social studies teacher was trying to find ways to bring more guest speakers to class, to get students out on field trips to apply course learnings, and to manage those activities with ''less hassle.''

Others on the staff were concerned about the impact (Stage 4) of their work on the student. Twenty years of research on the Concerns concept suggests that as people gain experience and knowledge and skill in relation to an innovation, consequence concerns become more intense (Hall and Rutherford, 1990, p. 23). Such an evolution of feelings would be consistent with maturing staffs like the ones at Bromley and Mansfield. Some Stage 4 concerns are

- A science teacher, integrating contemporary material into her course (e.g., genetic counseling, euthanasia, holistic health) said, ''Kids today need to be made aware of controversial issues.''
- An industrial arts teacher, wondering how to stimulate and sustain student interest in new material, observed, ''Their interest controls the whole thing. The more they're into it, the better it works for me.''

Given the individualistic, single-classroom pattern to instruction in schools, it is not surprising to see only one teacher at Stage 5, Collaboration, and none at the Refocusing level. This pattern was reinforced by the fact that neither Bromley nor Mansfield had staff development programs aimed at bringing teachers together in any consistent way to work on matters of curriculum and instruction, or to create innovations that would require staff interaction for implementation.

## The Principal's Role

Just as it appears that principal behavior had an impact on teachers' Level of Use of the innovation, the same appears to be the case for the concerns expressed by many teachers. Because the Bromley principal was not as much of an interventionist as the Mansfield principal, Bromley staff had to deal with more management concerns about voluntary innovations, while Mansfield teachers did not. Bromley staff did not feel that they received the help they needed. On a day-to-day basis, the Mansfield principal was more skilled at using the "one-legged conference" — any opportunity that presented itself — to check on teacher concerns. Hall and Hord allege, "Principals do not take advantage of these one-to-two minute conferences to monitor or facilitate change. All too often they become forgotten moments of informal exchanges of pleasantries" (1987, p. 63). Again, CBAM research demonstrates that when those who intervene target specific individual concerns, there is a greater likelihood that the person being helped will move to the next Stage of Concern [Hall and Rutherford, 1990, p. 24].

The feelings, attitudes, and perceptions surfaced through the open-ended "concerns" question show that change facilitators must understand and appreciate the subjective dimension of teaching — its phenomenology — before trying to get users to alter their current practices. This point has been made elsewhere in this book. In any organization, due to individual job assignments, distance grows between employees so that over time a lack of appreciation and understanding develops. Miles, after a detailed and instructive study of twelve National Diffusion Network innovations, concluded, "It was clear in our sites that administrators and teachers lived in separate worlds" (1983, p. 19; see also Huberman and Miles, 1984).

In good schools this separateness (between teachers and between teachers and administrators and others) is minimized. It can be decreased in various ways, such as through ongoing supervisory processes that take administrators into classrooms on a regular basis or through the "simple" practice of a principal serving periodically as a substitute teacher or even teaching a course as part of her assignment. Of course, these actions, although helpful in this respect, in themselves will not break down the separatist norms or lead to considerable staff collaboration.

### Stages of Concern (from questionnaires)

As was mentioned earlier, two mandated, organization-wide policy innovations were identified at Bromley and Mansfield – the Competency Regulations and Public Law 94-142 staffings.

In each school the mandates were met with less than an enthusiastic response, but each principal was clear and firm in the belief that the organization had a responsibility to implement these innovations, that compliance would be in good spirit, and that implementation would be done well. As Loucks and Zacchei put it, a key factor in school improvement efforts is an administrator who says, "We're going to do this together, and we're going to get all the help we need" (1983, p. 30).

To examine concerns associated with the competencies and staffings, I drew on the Stages of Concern questionnaire, a thirty-five-item, validated instrument.

In both schools, the English, mathematics, social studies, and science departments were responsible for implementing the regulations, for teaching and testing the competencies, and for keeping records. While the staffings could, in theory, affect every teacher, some teachers, due to their assignment (e.g., basic math or English versus calculus or French) had considerably more contact with lower achieving youngsters who had difficulty passing the competencies. Therefore, the SoC instrument was administered only to those staff involved in implementation. All staff who were asked to do so completed the questionnaire.

Processing the questionnaire responses resulted in a profile plotted on a grid that displays relatively "higher" and "lower" concerns. It is important to stress that higher or lower concerns are not synonymous with "good or bad" feelings. What the scores indicate is an individual's intensity of concern about an innovation at a moment in time. The higher the score, the stronger the feelings, attitudes, and perceptions. The most important aspect of the profiles is not how high or low they are on the grid, but the relative difference in the peaks and valleys.

Also, according to Concerns theory, a difference in intensity of at least ten percentile points is an "important" difference in concerns – important in that the concerns could be interfering with one's work and therefore need attending to. Outcomes from the questionnaires are displayed in Figures 6.2 and 6.3.

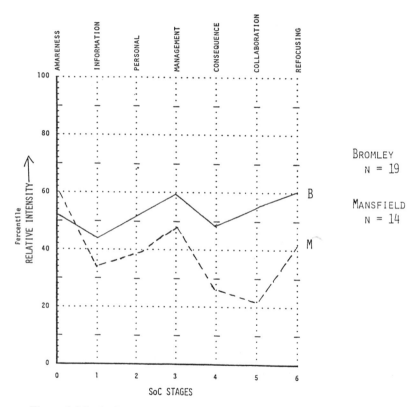

**Figure 6.2** Basic Competency Concerns of Bromley and Mansfield Teachers.

88

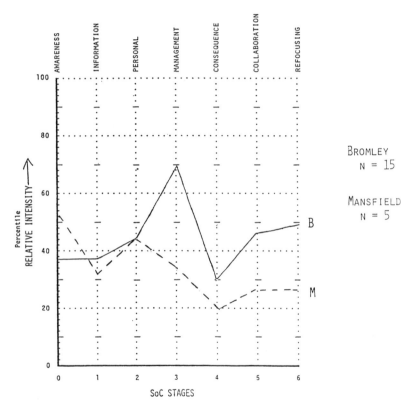

**Figure 6.3** Staffing Concerns of Bromley and Mansfield Teachers.

89

## Observations about the Profiles

The factors shown in Chart 6.1, drawn from interviews, documents, and limited observation, are offered as reasons for the differences in the SoC profiles.

### Chart 6.1—Basic Competencies (BCs)

| Bromley (N = 19) | Mansfield (N = 14) |
| --- | --- |
| — A three-page, detailed set of instructions on managing the competencies was available to staff, including how to record pupil progress. | — A one-page less detailed set of instructions was available which did not address items such as record keeping. |
| — Each department responsible for competency implementation had at least one teacher (some had two) assigned to a Competency Class in place of a regular class assignment. By using this period in combination with a regular unassigned period, a teacher was able to take youngsters out of study hall who were in need of more help with BCs. Teachers felt that they were able to contact "90 percent" of students in need of assistance. | — The English and math departments had a teacher assigned to a "lab" in place of a regular class assignment. This period was used similarly to what was done at Bromley. Teachers felt that there were still many students who they were not able to assist. |
| — Competency tests were in place in all departments responsible for BCs and were being used with results recorded. The principal used these results to follow up on problem students and to identify weak spots in the BC system. | — Tests were in place in English, math, and social studies and were being used with results recorded. The principal used these results similarly to the Bromley principal. |

| Bromley (N = 19) | Mansfield (N = 14) |
|---|---|
| — Each department was required to keep a BC file on each student for whom it had responsibility, which was used in combination with a once-a-year computer printout. A typical teacher comment was, "I trust them more than the printout as I *know* they are my entries." These were kept up to date and monitored periodically by the principal, who also monitored the system through printout data. | — Files were kept on a voluntary basis by the English, math, and social studies departments. Computer printouts were provided quarterly. The principal monitored the system through the printouts. |

### Staffings *

| Bromley (N = 19) | Mansfield (N = 14) |
|---|---|
| — Four pages of detailed instructions on placement procedures, staffing procedures and staffing protocol were available to staff. | — No written instructions were available to staff. |
| — The written material made it clear that any staff member identified as "regularly in contact" with the student was required to attend. Anyone not attending ". . . will be so noted for the record." | — "Required attendance" was stated verbally and in writing by the principal and the Resource Room teacher. |
| — Staffings were held before school, were limited strictly to thirty minutes, and were taped. People attending arrived on time and did not leave early. | — Staffings were held after school, often started late, and often ran over the set time frame. People attending sometimes arrived late and left early. |

*(continued)*

| Bromley (N = 19) | Mansfield (N = 14) |
|---|---|
| — The principal regularly chaired staffings. Of 106 staffings between January and October, he chaired 103. He once stated, "I take a trip every time we have a staffing. It is the one place where professionalism really comes through day after day." | — The principal only attended when requested by the Resource Room teacher. |
| — At least five days before a staffing, the Resource Room teacher notified, on paper, those people who were to attend. This notice instructed them to come prepared to discuss the strengths and weaknesses of the student and tentative recommendations. | — At least five days before a staffing, the Resource Room teacher notified, on paper, those people who were to attend. |
| — The Resource Room teacher was beginning to observe eligible students in regular classrooms on a systematic basis. | — There was no systematic observation of eligible students in regular classrooms. |
| — The Resource Room teacher was starting her third year full-time on the job. | — The Resource Room teacher was starting her first year full-time on the job. |

*The difference in the N's of teachers highly involved in staffings was due to these reasons:

(1) Although PL 94-142 requires only one staffing every three years on an eligible student, at Bromley they were held every year and any teacher who had that individual in class was required to be present. Therefore, many teachers in grades 9-12 were involved. There were also numerous requests for staffings from teachers.

(2) At Mansfield, because students were coming right from the three elementary schools into the 7th grade, the focus of early staffings was on junior high youngsters. Therefore, only those teachers were highly involved.

Clearly the management of these policy innovations had an important impact on teachers. In contrast to his reactive behavior toward the voluntary innovations in his school, the Bromley principal had a "game plan" for implementing these organizational level changes. The

Mansfield principal, in contrast to his initiating behavior toward his school's voluntary innovations, did not have as strong a "game plan" to guide his management of the competencies and staffings.

These outcomes are very much in line with the Huberman and Miles findings relative to National Diffusion Network and Title IV-C innovations. They found that the presence of a sound support system, plus active assistance to teachers by change facilitators (building and central office administrators), were prime factors in the successful implementation of the innovations. Support (in this instance from principals) took the form of ongoing contact between the facilitator and staffs, offers of help from the facilitator, and concrete assistance by her in the form of actions such as schedule modifications, assigning aides, obtaining resources, and offering solutions to problems (1984, pp. 88-114). This kind of leadership helped immensely in stabilizing the new programs and practices and led to their institutionalization.

Although the competencies and staffings were mandated for Bromley and Mansfield and thus would not "disappear," the differences in how they were being managed affected their organizational impact. If they had been voluntary changes, it seems very possible that those at Mansfield would have had less of a chance to survive than those at Bromley. These conclusions about the importance of managerial acts to successful change are consistent with other conclusions, addressed in Chapters 4 and 5, about the role of leadership. There are some things that only administrators can do, and while each individual administrative act may appear insignificant in the total scheme of things, to the change agent each is critical to success – even if they consist of relatively isolated incident interventions rather than game plans.

In addition to the impact of these management factors on the competencies and staffings, there were other reasons for the differences in their implementation.

First were human factors, such as the personnel available at that moment in organizational history who could assume added responsibilities. At Mansfield, a new Resource Room teacher was not too sure of herself when it came to running the staffings. Therefore, the less active involvement of the principal had a real impact on teacher concerns about staffings.

Second were managerial philosophies about the degree to which principals should be engaged in regular activities related to the implementation of mandated innovations. Given that these innovations did not meet the four criteria (described earlier) that Fullan identified as critical to successful implementation, it seems that the choice of philosophies should be on the side of more active intervention.

If administrators should be involved, then in what ways? The Bromley principal chose to intervene in several specific ways on a sustained basis, which contributed to "program settledness" or stabilization (Huberman and Miles, 1984, p. 126). Considering the special organizational characteristics of schools, in which teachers already expend considerable energy maintaining classroom control and dealing with myriad job details, creating a situation where they have to confront even more details and have their frustration levels raised—particularly regarding changes imposed on them—will have a negative impact on their attitude and motivation.

By becoming settled, the innovations increased the sense of efficacy felt by teachers. There was a decided difference between Bromley and Mansfield teachers, with those at Bromley feeling more comfortable, confident, in control, and gratified in relation to their use of the competencies and staffings. Interestingly, these four indicators of efficacy were present in the NDN and Title IV-C sites (Huberman and Miles, 1984, p. 115).

An interesting point at this juncture is that where the change facilitator chooses to focus his or her attention and energy can have a decided impact on implementation. In turn, it may well be that such choice making has more of an impact on the success of certain innovations than the importance of the innovation itself (in this instance, two mandates) (Hord, 1991).

Data from the Levels of Use and Stages of Concern support Berman's contention that two activities have been found to be frequently identified with successful implementation. The first is thoughtful adaptation, which is the tailoring of an innovation (which is not highly defined) to fit the local situation. At Bromley, according to CBAM data, adaptation was a more effective process. The second is clarification, which is how users become more clear about the nature of the innovation, its objectives, what is needed to make it work, and their role in the process (1981, pp. 271-273). With fairly broad policy innovations like the competencies and staffings, clarification emerged as the policies were gradually implemented. Again, this seemed to happen more effectively at Bromley than at Mansfield.

## INSTITUTIONALIZATION

Institutionalization, the third phase of the Rand framework, is when the innovation continues (i.e., when it has become a "permanent" part of the organization). Conditions are present that indicate that it has become routinized; despite the fact that the novelty has worn off there is no flagging of enthusiasm, which can push a good, new change aside in favor of old practices.

Huberman and Miles state that the ultimate measure of institutionalization is when members of the organization indicate that the innovation will eventually be revised, just like other programs or practices, in the normal cycle of organizational events (1984, p. 209). Loucks-Horsley and Hergert, drawing on the same data base of NDN studies, point out in their handbook for school improvement, that "Institutionalization does not just happen naturally. It takes planning and effort, often with the people who, up to this point, have not been part of the effort" (1985, p. 65).

We know from research that the press of everyday activities tends to cause behavior to regress to former routines, but it is difficult to determine when an innovation meets the conditions of continuation because this phase is the least studied of the three (Fullan, 1982, pp. 76-78; Larson, 1988, pp. 53-54).

Muddying things, too, is the fact that even if an innovation seems to have become institutionalized, it may get "shelved" permanently or temporarily, often due to the difficulty of using it or because it no longer seems to do the job it was intended to do. Voluntary innovations, if adopted or developed in a situation where there is little supervisory oversight, interest, or support shown to innovators who may want and need it, are particularly susceptible to gradual disuse. Critical here is staff development assistance because change agents often require more help at this phase than they do during mobilization and implementation. Research findings are firm in this conclusion (e.g., Huberman and Miles, 1984, pp. 255-258).

Finally, even when there is a formal organizational decision to discontinue an innovation, some employees may still use elements of it. Books, films, videotapes, computers, methods, and print materials of various kinds may all find a new home in the regular program within a teacher's workspace.

While the mandated innovations required planning and effort, as we have seen, voluntary innovations at Bromley and Mansfield—which we will look at next—demonstrated that institutionalization and discontinuation often "happen" in less than visible ways. At times these phases of change appear to be a naturally occurring process.

## Continuation

Other than the ten-year self-evaluation conducted in each school in preparation for a visit by a regional accreditation team, neither organization had developed a systematic means by which to decide what programs and practices should be retained.

As was discussed in Chapter 4, school philosophy and goals were not conscious reference points for mobilization decisions and neither were they for those relative to institutionalization.

Rather, these kinds of decisions presented themselves at various times, imbedded in choice situations and choice opportunities. Because these situations occurred on a "rolling basis" they are illustrative of the

> . . . complicated intermeshing of the mix of choices available at any one time, the mix of problems that have access to the organization, the mix of solutions, and the outside demands on the decision makers. [March and Olsen, 1979, p. 36]

Considering the work demands on the principals and teachers, it was next to impossible for them to find the time to engage in calculated, collaborative decisions about continuing or not continuing the many small-scale innovations existing in each school. The policy innovations were mandated to continue, but, as we saw earlier, there were real differences between the schools in how continuation was managed.

## Discontinuation

Over the five-year period that this study covered, through the initial seventy-eight exploratory interviews with administrators, counselors, special education personnel, and teachers, twenty-six courses were identified as having been eliminated at Bromley and twenty-three at Mansfield. Two curricular units had been dropped at Bromley. Teachers had a difficult time identifying anything that had been dropped.

The reasons given by interviewees for making decisions to eliminate a program or practice are as follows:

- material too difficult for students
- community discontent with electives
- enrollment decline
- loss of staff
- lack of student interest

- boring material, inability to get speakers, cost of film rentals
- students' procrastination in doing work
- community reaction to kids out in town during the day
- no time to do justice to material
- material covered in another class

### Observations about Discontinuation

Dropping an innovation may in itself be an innovative act and another indicator of organizational climate. Sometimes it is far more difficult to jettison a program or practice than it is to adopt or develop it, because if it has been used successfully for some time and is seen as a beneficial addition, users often come to have an investment in it. For example, a teacher who has developed an elective course may want to retain it, but the school board may decide that new required courses require a reduction in electives. In good schools, there is a willingness to look beyond these vested interests if it appears that programs and practices no longer serve the purposes of the organization.

In a high school, dropped courses can be tracked by examining programs of study from year to year. Structural innovations usually have to be scheduled and technological innovations can be observed. However, it is virtually impossible to track dropped units, themes, or methods and materials. Hence memory, which is not very reliable, becomes a key retrieval device. Considering the number of voluntary innovations identified at Bromley and Mansfield, it seems reasonable to conclude that over five years more things were discontinued than could be remembered in order to make room for the ''add-ons.''

In this situation, more courses were dropped than were added. The main reason for this was the elimination of numerous English and social studies electives in each school in favor of more required courses and fewer choices. Bromley and Mansfield were caught up in the national ''back to basics'' movement of the mid-1970s, and the osmotic process of change made these English and social studies courses prime targets of criticism for offering less than rigorous experiences for students.

Because courses are important change-bearing vehicles in secondary schools and have to be brought before the school board for approval or discontinuation, the principals played an active decision-making role in relationship to them. Some of the ''drop'' situations even involved ''bundles'' of several courses, and the board acted on them during a relatively short period of time. This dynamic is an illustration of Weick's contention that a major positive feature of loosely coupled organizations like schools is their adaptability.

> Loosely coupled systems can also adapt to small changes in an environment, especially when that environment is diverse and segmented. Departmental units that are free to vary independently may provide a more sensitive mechanism for detecting changes in the environment, and they allow the school to adapt quickly to conflicting demands. [1982, p. 674]

Course drops and adds did not occur on a one-to-one match. In some cases, content was simply eliminated from a curriculum or in other cases it was integrated into other courses. For example, content from an introduction to physical science course was integrated into basic chemistry, physics, and biology, and American government was absorbed partially into U.S. History. Such processes enabled many such decisions to be made with minimal disruption to the rest of the school. They show that adaptability works in many subtle ways.

The findings about phenomena of implementation and institutionalization, and findings relative to mobilization, demonstrate that change is very much a process and not an event; that it is accomplished primarily by individuals; that it is a highly personal experience; that it entails developmental growth; that it is best understood in operational terms; that the focus of change facilitation should be on individuals, innovations, and the context; and that leadership plays a central role throughout all three phases of change. The findings also demonstrate that details revolving around most innovative activities are numerous and sometimes nearly overwhelming. Therefore, a theory of changing offers the best hope for becoming more effective across various change situations rather than attempting to develop a personal lexicon of highly rational prescriptions that can be pulled out of a kit for application at a specific time and place.

# Small Wins: The Potential for School Improvement

> A small win is a concrete, complete, implemented outcome of moderate importance. By itself, one small win may seem unimportant. A series of small wins at small but significant tasks, however, reveals a pattern that may attract allies, deter opponents, and lower resistance to subsequent proposals. Small wins are controllable opportunities that produce visible results. [Weick, 1984, p. 43]

This book has described, in considerable detail from a cultural perspective, the factors and phenomena connected to small-scale innovation. It has also described the factors and phenomena connected to larger-scale innovation as uncovered through application of the Concerns-Based Adoption Model. Building on them, I have aimed to help you, the reader, develop or refine your working theory of change from the inside out.

Although most of what has been described has focused on the high school, it is also highly applicable to elementary and middle schools in urban, suburban, or rural settings.

What has been discussed is very much in line with Cuban's first-order type of change, which was mentioned in Chapter 1. In all probability, small wins in themselves will not lead to fundamental, second-order alterations in goals, structures, roles, curriculum, or instruction. However, schools like Bromley and Mansfield, which possess the capability to be adaptable and to renew themselves, can become far more effective by using a strategy of small wins.

I agree with Ravitch who, after an extensive analysis of school improvement efforts, 1945-1980, concluded that "piecemeal," incremental change may be the more sensible route to changing schools because of the decentralized nature and particular organizational features of schools (1983, p. 261). Some researchers with the Coalition of Essential Schools are beginning to place increased value on small-scale innovation (*Horace*, November 1990). But will that approach satisfy the critics who are calling for dramatic reform and restructured organizations?

Consider some observations about school reform movements since the 1960s which come from the Rand Corporation study discussed in Chapter 1. The authors, Elmore and McLaughlin, point out that reformers have not learned many lessons from the history of educational change and, because they have not, most current policy-type change efforts—efforts that focus on goals and curriculum content, improving the quality of teaching and the organization of schools, and upgrading standards for student performance—will "unravel" too (1988, pp. 53-62). The reforms will very likely unravel because increased numbers of innovations are today being imposed on schools, just as they have been during other periods of "outside in" improvement, yet the organizational structures and the work loads of staff have remained the same.

While not all the proposals for improvement are inherently flawed, those that are not, by and large, will not work as intended. Policy is by nature a "blunt instrument" whose implementation requirements are quite disconnected from practice. These requirements often cannot accommodate organizational variability, and too often higher authority is given precedence over local judgment, competence, and expertise.

> Instead of reforming and renewing schools from the inside out, school people will be given the task of translating competing and often unreasonable demands into practical solutions that may or may not be consistent with effective practice. [Elmore and McLaughlin, 1988, p. 60]

Sarason [1990] is an outright pessimist about the probability for success of the current wave of reforms. He contends that until we confront the deep-rooted social, institutional, and organizational obstacles prevalent in schools, most reforms will fail. Many of these obstacles are connected to the nature of the school as an organization portrayed in Chapter 3. For him, power relationships between teachers and students, teachers and administrators, and schools and parents are a key to reform, yet altering them in fundamental ways is extremely difficult, making schools "intractable" to startling innovations.

Although the pace of state-enacted policy innovations of the above types has slowed today compared to the mid-1980s (Futrell, 1989, p. 11), the most popular current reform strategy, sometimes promulgated at the state level, is the site-managed school. One encounters the concept (see Chapter 4) in virtually every professional journal and it is even on the lips of national, state, and local politicians. Unlike past broad, diffuse goals of "back to the basics," "humanize education," "equity," or "excellence," this strategy is very specific—the bottom line to change is the local organization, where there will be different patterns to the way schools are governed by the public and educators.

However, logic says that more site management responsibilities will add to the already hectic and pressed work pace existing in schools. With such responsibility comes increased demand on the time of administrators, teachers, counselors, special educators, and other personnel. Time will become an issue because today's norms call for participatory decision making through committees and councils of all kinds, involving varying configurations of school personnel, parents, and other relevant groups. That process demands many extra hours out of personal schedules, more than most educators find in the press of the day-to-day operation.

As an example, recently a principal told me how difficult she and her staff found it to address real substantive curricular and instructional issues in their school because the union contract allowed for only one faculty meeting a month—on Monday from 3:00 to 4:00 P.M. In another school I worked with recently during an inservice day in October, the staff's next scheduled time together for schoolwide development purposes was early March.

This lack of regular, significant time for these kinds of activities is an enormous drag on the pace of change. Yet most schools face formidable obstacles in trying either to extend the school year to include more inservice days (in this case, contractual) or to take more time from the regular schedule for such purposes (working parents complain about child sitting problems or about the fact that cutting into "time on task" flies in the face of current external pressures to cover more content).

Involvement in organizational governance also requires time for training in communications and decision-making skills if educators and lay people are to work together effectively. Such collaboration is not easy to achieve in any situation, but it is compounded in the case of schools because administrators and teachers have been educated on a psychological "independent agent" model (see the Introduction) and teachers, once employed, are accustomed to working independently of colleagues. Even with training in processes, great effort must be made to overcome the traditions that counteract group cooperation and collaboration.

In addition, many board members and parents have little or no background working in group situations through mainly participative processes. Several days ago I visited a school that is making great strides in improving itself. But the principal described his frustration over the ineffectiveness of the board chair, who has limited skills at running meetings and is resistant to obtaining them through any kind of training program. Meetings drag on after midnight with the agenda often not covered, and even when it is, poor decisions often result. He is concerned that good members, already frustrated, will not run for office again. He is also frustrated because of the lack of effort on the part of his superintendent to try to intervene with the chair and help him become more effective. In this case, the principal, unlike the principals of Bromley and Mansfield, has not been delegated responsibility to work directly with the chair.

Unions and management in some communities are beginning to recognize the need to alter these norms and working conditions, rooted in the adversarial model of bargaining, in order to take serious steps toward reform. Both the American Federation of Teachers and the National Education Association are engaged in innovative contract experiments in several districts that represent significant new thrusts in regard to decision making and participatory management, thrusts that address long-standing issues relating to roles, authority, responsibility, accountability, and time for teachers to engage in substantive tasks. These experiments are taking teachers, administrators, and boards into uncharted waters that all parties must learn to navigate well if site-managed schools are really to work (Watts and McClure, 1990; Tuthill, 1990; and Rauth, 1990).

Although there is a lot of shared decision making in good schools, despite current constraints, what is being called for in that regard today (exemplified by the new union contract experiments discussed above) goes way beyond that level in intensity and frequency.

If site management is to assist the goal of moving toward second-order change, then it may well require additional staff to reduce instructional workloads (and here I have not discussed the increased time and psychological demands on teachers to respond to needs to implement more individualized programs, to utilize cooperative group learning techniques, and to integrate more children with handicaps into regular classrooms). Also, as we have seen from the change research, larger-scale innovations require some kind of oversight from administrators, yet these new site management demands will divert time toward process activities. In theory, then, administrators too need more assistance, yet the clear trend nationwide is to reduce the size of instructional and management staffs. Confronted with the financial situation before us, hiring more staff is a remote possibility; hence to achieve these goals the only alternative seems to be to redesign the system to promote new patterns of school organization. The flavor of the new union contracts may be a taste of what could come over the next few years in these regards.

If more time is not provided or some kind of redesign achieved, ''burn out'' will prevent educators from meeting the expectations for what should happen in a site-managed organization. Failure to site-manage effectively and to have that site management result in noticeably improved learning will result in public disenchantment and redoubled demands for voucher and choice plans. Already the Bush administration has established, within the Department of Education, a Center for Choice in Education which will be an information clearinghouse to aid the growing interest in the idea (Pitsch, 1990, p. 30), and in its fiscal 1992 budget has included a $200-million fund for grants to districts that have established parental choice policies (Pitsch, 1991, p. 29).

Proponents of site-based management face other challenges. How will schools in the same district coordinate and articulate their programs while maintaining building autonomy? How will autonomous schools deal with district and sometimes building-level union contracts; with changed roles among administrators, teachers, boards, parents, and even students; and with increased demands for more financial resources and ways to reallocate existing resources?

Given current and projected economic conditions, there is little possibility that the 1990s will see significant new funds for schools to further the goals of the site-based movement or enable researchers to conduct studies of the above issues. As David (1989) puts it in her synthesis of the studies on the subject, most of the unanswered questions will be answered through experimentation, and we will learn from the mistakes and the successes. Clearly we will have to do better with what we have and do it without the guidance that comes from thorough analyses of what is happening in practice.

## RESTRUCTURING

Emerging from a site-managed organization, as numerous critics and policymakers see it, is ''restructured'' education. ''Restructuring'' has suddenly largely replaced "reform" and "renewal" as the popular term capturing a variety of expectations for school improvement. It is on the covers of professional journals and carries a high profile among national, state, and local policymakers. David Tyack, the noted educational historian, says that "As U.S. education enters the 1990s, *restructuring* has become a magic incantation" (1990, p. 170).

The term conveys an expectation of second-order change, and no doubt that is the general expectation in the minds of most of those who promote it. For example, a report on education released at the 1990 annual meeting of the National Governor's Association, asserts: "We need dramatic and fundamental changes in the way we design and structure education if we are to compete globally and achieve economic success" (Branstad quoted in Olson, 1990, p. 7).

In Vermont in 1991, where restructuring is being promoted by the State Board of Education and the Department of Education, virtually every administrator I have talked with during the last few months asserts that his/her school is "restructuring." Sample conversations with teachers confirm that the concept had entered the ethos of many classrooms too. I am amazed at how quickly it has spread. To use Weick's term, school people are highly "aroused" by talk about restructuring and by stories of neighboring organizations that are engaged in some restructuring activity. Shortly we will see what the concept means in practice to most educators.

On one level, restructuring fits with the notion of broad reform. It is an interesting example of osmotic change—something that just began to creep into the literature and the public agenda in the late 1980s, gradually replacing "reform" in the jargon lexicon. Tyack describes this dynamic very effectively in his analysis of sea changes in public education over the last century (1990). It is next to impossible to identify the exact origins of "restructuring." Are its roots in "perestroika?" Newspapers and magazines carry many stories today about restructuring in business and industry and in local and state government. One recent example in the public sector is the effort by the new Governor of Massachusetts to blend business practices with age-old government practices so that state government will be "reinvented," and emerging will be a new form of "entrepreneurial government" (Osborne, 1991, p. 65). It seems that, in general terms, restructuring is connected to crises, to questions of organizational or institutional survival.

In *Restructuring America's Schools*, a major overview of the movement, no one definition is offered but the themes convey what proponents advocate: changing the nature of schools from the interior; creating new relationships for children and teachers; examining our basic beliefs about teaching, learning, the nature of human beings, and the kinds of environments that maximize growth for teachers and students alike; and opening up the process of learning and teaching, of human interaction and decision making (Lewis, 1989, pp. 3-6). These goals contrast considerably with those of policymakers who, as we saw in Chapter 1, focus more on state legislation and regulations relating to higher academic standards, on recognition of teachers and ways to reward teachers, and on higher standards for those entering the profession.

Is, then, "reform" synonymous with "restructuring"? Timar concluded, after a national survey of the restructuring movement, that there is little agreement regarding what it means, what it looks like in practice, and how it should be implemented. At minimum it is a reform strategy (1989, p. 266).

In operational terms, what does restructuring seem to mean to practitioners in the field? A sample of programs and approaches from various projects around the country demonstrates that those who wrestle daily with the realities of delivering education to youth in classrooms see the concept as concrete and practical.

Those involved in the "Coalition of Essential Schools" focus on how students learn and how teachers teach in secondary schools. Major objectives of that project include finding ways to get students to "work" more at the task of learning; reducing content covered in favor of more depth of study; making learning more personalized; and assessing learning more effectively (see various issues of *Horace* and "The Common Principles of the Coalition of Essential Schools"). If all these objectives could be achieved, then, from my perspective, the school would be restructured because fundamental alteration would have occurred in traditional patterns of curriculum and instruction and in how students and teachers relate to one another.

A national survey of high school improvement projects revealed major emphasis on topics such as increasing staff responsibility for solving school problems, increasing parental support for schools, publicizing academic achievement, and curriculum development (Purkey, Rutter, and Newmann, 1986, pp. 68-71). ''Successful'' schools identified under the U.S. Department of Education's Recognition Program relied on these kinds of innovations (Wilson and Corcoran, 1988, pp. 119-129), as did ''restructuring'' schools surveyed by the National Education Association (*NEA Today*, September 1990, pp. 4-5). From my perspective, these kinds of changes, although worthy, would be more at the level of renewal and perhaps reform because the basic features of the organization would remain quite the same.

A current example of what many educators would call restructuring (and I concur) is the shift from junior high to middle school, especially in the last decade. Rather than identifying themselves as preparatory schools for high school, middle schools see themselves as separate organizations uniquely suited to serve the pre-adolescent student. The true middle school attempts to address the learning, physical, and psychological growth needs of its clientele through innovations such as teacher-advisors and mentors; a more interdisciplinary curriculum that provides students with many opportunities for exploration and experimentation; team-teaching through block-scheduling of core subjects; cooperative grouping and cross-age tutoring; flexibility in scheduling; and a program that balances cognitive learning, self-esteem, values, and personal development issues (*Turning Points*, 1989).

Finally, Carroll has proposed ''The Copernican Plan,'' an exciting vision for a radically different way to reorganize the high school based on a totally different schedule aimed at promoting more individualized instruction and more mastery of learning (1990, pp. 358-365).

Do these innovations constitute ''small change,'' mere tinkering with the status quo? Or will they meet the expectations of the reformers who are calling for restructured education? Is there a real danger that schools will again be caught in a crossfire of highly conflicting hopes?

To my knowledge, the most instructive lessons about attempting to restructure secondary schools emerged from the Model Schools Project of the National Association of Secondary Schools Principals (outlined in Chapter 2). It was an attempt to alter significantly, through a very well researched and well designed model, the way that junior and senior high schools were structured, how instruction was delivered, and how youth learned.

Since I was affiliated with the project as a site visitor to several of the schools, I observed first-hand how they struggled in the context of ''organized anarchy'' and ''busy kitchen'' environments to succeed with a combination of team-teaching, differentiated staffing, flexible scheduling, learning activity packages, new roles for professionals, and various methods to individualize instruction.

Of the thirty schools that initially were in the "Trump Project," only three or four were able to truly become "model schools." What could account for the overall lack of success in what appeared to be a promising approach to restructuring? Administrative turnover, difficulties of showing fairly quickly that certain innovations were having a clear positive impact on learning, thin financial resources, community opposition, and simplistic views on the part of educators and boards as to what it would take to make the total program work—these elements led to the demise of the approach in most schools (Trump and Georgiades, 1977, pp. 72-79). It is disappointing to note that, to my knowledge, nowhere in any of the 1980s reports and studies about secondary schools is there reference to this important project. This is an example of Elmore and McLaughlin's and Sarason's observations about not learning from experience, and yet the reasons for the project's difficulties are disturbingly parallel to present factors swirling around many restructuring efforts (see Timar, 1989) and ones that undermined other innovative programs and practices described elsewhere in this book.

Restructuring is an admirable goal that has considerable potential conceptually to shift our thinking about change and to move us to actions that can improve schools in important ways. However, presently it is defined differently by various groups, which does not bode well for its future. As educators we have a responsibility to understand these definitional differences, to educate other groups about them, and to get agreement at the local level, at least among professionals and boards, about the meaning of the term. Otherwise we could again get mired in a morass of clashing expectations that would divert our attention and energy from the real issues, possible solutions, and support needed to implement them.

The focus of this book, with the exception of Chapter 6, has been on "small wins"—a strategy for change that can work now in all schools, quite apart from issues relating to economic resources or local social-political conditions. While clearly we need, in most situations, a serious rethinking about existing curriculum and the very nature of instruction, combined with ambitious comprehensive change if we are to truly reform and perhaps restructure public education, enormous dollars (to name just one factor) are required to underwrite such an effort. Rather than wait for them to be forthcoming, we must forge ahead with our school improvement efforts, taking other approaches that may not fit the textbook prescriptions for more orderly, farsighted change. Small wins are a key to adaptability and to the continuous organizational renewal described in Chapter 2.

# Levers and Footings for Change

The best course may be a middle course. One approach would be to encourage incremental reforms by using schools such as those described in this book as natural laboratories while also supporting limited and carefully designed experiments with new organizational forms. [Wilson and Corcoran, 1988, p. 147]

In the pages preceding this chapter, research is cited regarding the difficulty of effecting large-scale change. Given that fact, along with the evidence that it is possible to bring about smaller-scale change fairly readily, in this section of this last chapter I will describe some "levers for improvement" that, in my experience, can be used fairly quickly – in many instances with a modicum of reading, thought, and preparation but requiring a considerable dash of common sense. Use of them could encourage more rapid incremental change, as Wilson and Corcoran conclude is possible in the schools they studied, which were recognized as excellent schools under the U.S. Department of Education's Recognition Program (Mansfield was one of those 571 schools).

The "levers" are in no order of import or potential impact. Their use is highly contextual in terms of the condition of the local site. All can be used separately for some purposes, and many can be combined with others into a mosaic of strategies. No doubt readers, from their experiences, can add to the list.

## LEVERS FOR IMPROVEMENT

### Mosaics of Small-Scale Innovations

Although they can be free-standing innovations in most instances, the components of the Model Schools Project and the middle school movement do fit together in a logical, coherent pattern. They are an example of how a mosaic of innovations can have far more impact on the organization than these innovations would have singly. Thus, calculated "small change" could lead to a very different school if a design is seen among the parts.

This corresponds with what Weick (1985) refers to as "small stable segments" within the larger organization. Because they are parts of the whole, they are not necessarily disorderly and unconnected to each other any more than are sentences within paragraphs. Weick goes on to say, "Instead, what seems to be true within organizations is that coherence occurs in smaller sized entities than may be true in other settings" (p. 117). Such appears to be the case in the "excellent" businesses described by authors like Kanter (1983) and Peters and Waterman (1982) where small-scale change was a key to their effectiveness and competitiveness. Waterman, in *The Renewal Factor*, devotes several pages to explicitly discussing the value of "tiny steps" (1987, p. 245).

The most detailed picture of this process of change emerged from Kouzes' and Posner's study of excellent businesses. They state,

> A series of small wins therefore provides a foundation of stable building blocks. Each win preserves gains and makes it harder to return to pre-existing conditions. Like miniature experiments or pilot studies, small wins also provide information that facilitates learning and adaptation. [1987, p. 221]

The book describes several ideas about management and leadership such as continuous experimentation; dividing tasks into manageable chunks; reducing the essence of the "win" to its essentials; and building, obtaining, and sustaining commitment to a course of action.

Guskey (1990) has proposed several guidelines for "integrating innovations" that can be applied to create a connectedness between small-scale changes. These deal with goal and strategy compatibility, the recognition that no one innovation can do everything, and adaptability to local conditions. He contends that by using a set of innovations, far more improvement can occur in a shorter period of time than is usually the case when focusing on one or two major innovations. A mosaic strategy is similar to this approach.

Finally, the mosaic strategy fits nicely into the notion of evolutionary planning as derived by Louis and Miles (1990) from their study of five urban high schools. In that process, small-scale innovations play a key role because there is more certainty that they will be implemented successfully. That success increases motivation and stimulates further action (pp. 209-216).

## Planning

The traditional framework of planning is seen as keying off of system and subsystem goals with subsequent organizational activities occurring in a sequential, highly structured, and quite predictable pattern. Although research about planning, as well as the use of the ideal process in schools, has not produced the kind of success that encourages us to place great credence in the activity, the outcomes—from my perspective as discussed in Chapter 5—do not support the notion that what we then do is "irrational."

There is strong evidence that we are often driven by rational reasons other than the desire to attain system goals, reasons linked integrally to attitudes, values, and feelings. Behavior is intentional but influenced considerably by affective forces. Waterman has recognized this fact in his study of the factors connected to renewal in the private sector. He concludes that planning may be important in itself because the process promotes communication, information sharing, and an atmosphere of "informed opportunism" and invention (1987, pp. 26-76).

Recently, some important new directions have been taken by students of educational planning that begin to chart a new course, one that attends to the affective dimensions of change. These directions show considerable promise for school professionals who need help in planning effectively within the context of the complex internal and external environments that influence schools.

One of the fresh approaches is the melding by Du Four and Eaker (1987) of findings from the effective schools literature with relevant findings from the literature about excellent businesses. They focus on the building level and provide specific strategies in combination with real-life examples.

Another approach comes from Carlson and Awkerman (1991), who tackle the challenge of applying strategic and operational planning concepts and practices to schools. They discuss critical issues relating to both traditional and emerging approaches to planning, factors in the organizational culture that affect planning, and the impact of policy-making on planning in schools. They also provide several instructive case studies that examine the application of strategic and operational planning at the district and state levels.

A third important book is *Improving the Urban High School* (1990). Louis and Miles focus on improvement/change issues but also address the aforementioned notion of evolutionary planning, which is very practical and applicable to all types of schools.

A fourth contribution, by authors like Cook (1990), McCune (1986), and Kaufman and Herman (1991), is the highly useful adaptation of strategic planning from the private sector to education. Here analyses of environmental trends and issues become a base for pushing the organization into desired future directions.

### Trend Analyses and Issue Identification

Schools too seldom look seriously and systematically at the future. Rarely have I encountered a school that builds into its schedule a regular time to examine societal and educational trends and their implications for curriculum, instruction, learning, and the way "business" is done. Yet social, economic, political, and cultural change swirls around us, as we saw in Chapter 1. Trend analysis is a basic element of strategic planning and can be initiated through "simple steps" such as staff reading of professional and popular journals, observations of the local community and workplace, and observations of what is conveyed through other media. Scenarios can be written. Later, outcomes can be linked more intentionally to other dimensions of strategic planning.

One way to begin to look at trends might be to look first at local issues that reflect trends. The school district in my community uses an annual survey of staff to identify key issues that will be addressed through staff development initiatives. The survey has led to programs about at-risk youth and their families, new trends in curriculum and instruction, the integration of regular and special education students and programs, and staff wellness concerns (South Burlington School District Staff Development Plan, 1989). Each school has a planning team composed of teachers, the counselor, and the principal, which assesses the degree to which the issue affects their school and how to respond to it. What is yet to be done is to take these issues and place them more in a futures context relating to broader trends. As a participant in a university-school partnership meeting put it the other day, "We need ways to dream beyond where we are."

## Derived Goals

Although research shows that organizational goals, as currently used, are not very important factors in planning and changing in most schools (e.g., Boyer, 1983, p. 61; Larson, 1982), we must still work at finding ways to give them utility. We must do so for at least four reasons.

(1) By nature, we are goal-seeking, goal-motivated creatures. We do not want to live and work in an environment that we perceive as directionless. If we feel that the system has no goals, then our personal goals become dominant and these goals may or may not mesh with what the system is trying to accomplish in fulfilling its societal mission. There is a constant tension in organizations between personal and organizational goals.

(2) Goals can help to create a different future. If we merely extrapolate from present individual action, then the chances are high that our future will be quite similar to our present, unless the organizational context orchestrates the movement of individual goals in a more common direction. "If the image of a potential future is convincing and rationally persuasive to men in the present, the image may become part of the dynamics and motivation of present action" (Chin and Benne, 1976, p. 30).

(3) Goals focus the mission and vigor of an organization. As we saw in Chapter 1, schools feel such intense pressure to assume so many tasks that they lose their sense of direction. As English puts it, "Organizations have limited resources. Survival requires them to focus their resources on certain activities to the exclusion of others" (1987, p. 26). Explicit goals would not automatically do this, but they could help greatly in keeping the school on course.

(4) Finally, it is simply poor public relations for a school to have no functional, stated goals. Possessing goals is so imbedded in the traditional definition of an organization and in the public's understanding of what an organization is all about that it is, in reality, an article of faith (Georgiou, 1973). To respond to the questioner who asks, "What are your goals?" by replying, "We don't have any," is risky business, considering the vulnerability of schools to their external constituencies as discussed in Chapter 3.

So we must continue to search for useful ways to set goals and to use them. Although logic says that we should arrive at our goals before we act, we know, as was described in Chapters 4 and 5, that schools act for reasons that are not attached so consciously to organizational goals. Therefore, why not develop a means to tap into what people are doing and to at least identify operational goals? Louis and Miles offer some provocative ideas about "action before planning" and "vision building" (1990, pp. 199-238). Taking an "innovation inventory" would be another means to identify operational goals. Then a discussion could be initiated regarding the desirability of being guided by these goals rather than by others. Out of such processes might emerge statements of mission that increasingly are seen in the recent planning literature as useful devices to focus attention and energy.

## Innovation Inventories and Catalogs of Innovations

Schools could, once a year, survey their staffs to identify the kinds of innovations that have been implemented and those that have been discontinued. Certainly the small-scale changes described in Chapter 4 are not very visible even to immediate peers, much less to administrators. I discovered this when I shared my findings with the principals of Bromley and Mansfield, and noted how surprised they were to hear about all the innovations effected by teachers beyond new courses (which they had to approve). The results of such a survey could provide a rich data base for discussion and insights about the "health" of the organization, could serve as a motivator in terms of local achievement, and could serve as a stepping stone for the examination of goals. What to some people appear to be minor or trivial accomplishments are actually small wins of real importance to organizational members. "Large-scale problems seem inpenetrable, whereas incremental steps are both doable and consistently rewarding" (Waterman, 1987, p. 261).

Related to conducting an internal inventory is the notion of conducting an external survey of possible innovations appropriate to meeting organizational needs. There is no dearth of ideas and concrete innovations available to schools, as is illustrated by Figure 8.1. As one of my graduate students put it recently, "My cup is full. I wish that someone would turn off the spigot for a while so that I could think about what I'm doing and how to do it better." I have heard similar comments from practitioners, many of whom feel almost "psychically paralyzed" by all the information swirling around them and their schools.

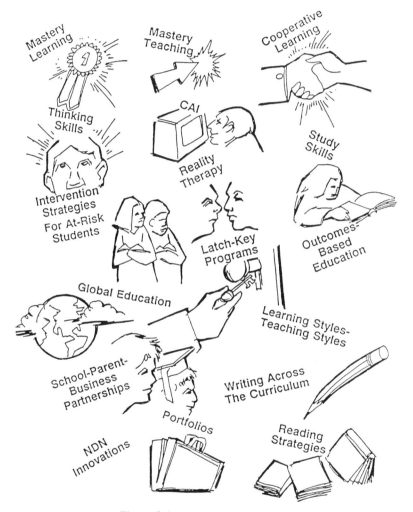

**Figure 8.1** A Catalog of Innovations.

115

"Educational Programs That Work" is one example of a prime source of well-developed, tested, and judged innovations, some 400 of them to date. The ERIC system is another useful national source. Convention programs abound with descriptions and demonstrations of innovations. Professional journals usually include articles outlining new programs, new technology, new processes of instruction, or new approaches to learning. Books have been developed based on collections of "prototypes that work" (Elam, 1989).

Despite the availability of all this information, many educators remain unaware of innovations that could be helpful to their organizations. Too often I hear, "I don't have time to read." There will never be enough time; as professionals we have a responsibility to schedule a few hours periodically to read and think about what is relevant to our work. As study findings revealed, the "simple" act of reading by the principals and teachers of Bromley and Mansfield resulted in many dividends for their schools. Numerous conversations with educators around the country, plus encounters with graduate students, indicate that many of them do not know about the National Diffusion Network, despite the fact that it has been in existence since 1974, and many do not know about key journals such as the *Phi Delta Kappan* and *Educational Leadership*. Too seldom do I find journals such as these on coffee tables in teacher's rooms in schools I visit.

We can take some initial steps to get informed through low-cost means of subscribing and talking. After that, additional lines of information gathering can be opened. The education profession does not do a good job of instilling the value of lifelong professional reading into undergraduate programs. This is but one dimension of teacher preparation programs that leads Lortie to conclude that they are not as intellectually demanding as are those of the more established professions (1975, p. 58). Therefore, as was discussed in Chapter 3, when it comes to change situations, work experience is valued more than knowledge derived from research and education.

## Idea Forums and Research Seminars

Schools need to create norms for pausing to share ideas and discuss research. Such exchange could take place with or without the assistance of external experts. As we saw in Chapter 4, the motivation to be "enlightened" is a powerful stimulant to change. As this drive gathers momentum among several staff, their example will cause stragglers to acquire the habit. While reading itself is a prime source of new knowledge and ideas for change, discussing what has been read is a vital step to making the habit pay off for organizational improvement.

In 1989, the National Council of Teachers of Mathematics published its "Curriculum and Evaluation Standards for School Mathematics." Given time and motivation for reading and exchange, schools could use this excellent document to help examine their mathematics curriculum. It describes societal changes that demand significant alterations in the way mathematics is taught, its content, where that content should be placed in the curriculum, and what content should be learned by what groups of children and youth. *Turning Points*, the middle school study referred to earlier, is another example of this kind of national publication.

Similarly, educators need to alter their often indifferent attitudes toward research and begin to value it as a vital tool for school improvement. While it is true that the checkered history of research has given practitioners little reason to place much faith in it as a tool for decision making, research is changing for the better. So although good schools may have some skepticism about research, they are learning to value it nevertheless and find ways to discuss it and, in some instances, make decisions based on it.

Johnson City, New York, is an excellent example of a district that gives research a high profile. The system, dealing with a high poverty rate, a new immigrant population, and limited financial resources, has developed a highly touted "outcomes-based" approach to education at all levels. It is the only district-level program approved for inclusion in the annual edition of "Educational Programs That Work," the publication of exemplary programs by the National Diffusion Network (1990).

Vickery, who conducted a study of the program, found that "school board policy requires all decisions to be based on the best research literature available" (1988, p. 54; see also Vickery, 1990). A few years ago I visited Johnson City and came away impressed with many things, especially with the way that research was respected by school staff members, and the way it was so integral to school improvement efforts. It was refreshing, too, to find the superintendent and the principals providing leadership to make research respectable and usable.

An important accompanying benefit of forums and seminars is that they would help to break down the separatist norms and barriers to interaction that exist in most schools. New norms of collegiality, collaboration, and teamwork are not formed overnight; they must be achieved through a commitment to meet with peers, to expose one's ideas, values, attitudes, and feelings, to work through conflict, and to strive toward creating different expectations for and patterns of behavior.

## Test Data

Most schools spend considerable time giving standardized tests, yet many do not use the data for other than public relations purposes. Over the years I have found it far too common to hear educators say, "Yes, we gave the Metropolitan Achievement Tests this year as we have every year I have worked here, but teachers have yet to see the results. To my knowledge they are somewhere in the principal's office. It's like they were dropped in a black hole."

How much more sensible it would be to distribute the information and use it to identify patterns of responses and consequent possible weak spots in the curriculum and maybe even in instruction. Such feedback could be a prod for change.

## School Report Cards

Educators can also issue "report cards" that inform the citizenry about the status of education in the community. The first district in Vermont to do this had a "School Report Night" in the fall of 1989. Its "report card" presented data about the family types of graduating seniors, poverty rates in local communities, enrollments and trends, average class sizes, staff-student ratios, staff demographics and salary profiles, average incomes in local communities, per-pupil costs, tax rates, local financial resources, standardized test scores, graduating senior plans, and dropout rates (Addison Northeast Supervisory Union, 1989). Several other districts are planning to issue report cards during 1990-91. The stimulus for change offered by this activity is obvious.

## Curriculum Auditing and Management

Other approaches that can stimulate school improvement, in the same way as can the use of test data and report cards, are curriculum auditing and management. They all focus initially on what is going on *now* and are constructed around the premise that before one can (or ought) to change, one must have a better understanding about present conditions. Auditing and management are illustrations of the emerging recognition in the research literature of the integral relationship between a well-run organization and innovation.

No organization should function under conditions such as those described by one of my workshop participants:

> Staff perform their assignments without a written curriculum guide, textbook sequence, departmental organization, grade level coordination, or planned communication among themselves.

Auditing, as developed by English (1988), is an adaptation of financial auditing and uses five broad standards relating to:

(1) Resources, programs, and personnel
(2) Goals and objectives
(3) Written plans and policies
(4) Use of program and student assessment data for adjusting, improving, or terminating programs
(5) Educational results and related costs

Curriculum management, a more focused dimension of auditing that hones in on curriculum practices, is structured around the key concepts of the written, taught, and tested curricula; quality control of curriculum; and curriculum alignment (English, 1987). While excessive application of auditing and management practices can easily lead to a "hyperrationalization" of change (described in Chapter 2), each can be equally liberating in terms of helping to establish a sense of organizational control and direction.

## FOOTINGS FOR CHANGE

Whether use of the "levers" results in real improvement depends heavily on the organizational conditions under which they are employed. Like the footings for a building, footings for change are critical to stability and organizational renewal, but it may be difficult to recognize their presence or absence. To determine such, one must be a good listener and observer.

### Organizational Climate

One of the quickest routes to changing schools is to alter organizational climate. The well-researched project of the National Association of Secondary Schools Principals concluded,

> The climate of a social environment is formed by the norms, beliefs, and attitudes reflected in the conditions, events, and practices of a particular environment. In this context, climate refers to prevailing or normative conditions which are relatively enduring over time and which can be used to distinguish one environment over another. [Kelley, 1980, p. 2]

A positive environment, as the Phi Delta Kappa project puts it, ''. . . makes a school a place where both staff and students want to spend a substantial portion of their time; it is a good place to be'' (Howard, Howell, and Brainard, 1987, p. 5). A distinguishing feature of good schools is the health of their organizational climates. That was true for Bromley and Mansfield and for other good schools mentioned in Chapter 4.

A negative climate can sap employee (and student) attitudes, morale, and motivation, as well as interest in reform and willingness to change. It can sour parent and board attitudes about the school and its personnel. Over the years, as I have worked in various ways with schoolpeople around the country, comments such as the following illustrate how certain behaviors and attitudes (in this case on the part of administrators) can affect climate.

- None of my administrators has ever asked what it is that I do, nor has anyone asked to see my curriculum notebook—and I've been in this school for ten years.
- I receive no verbal recognition, have little status in the organization, and little chance for career advancement. I have no one to share my successes and problems with and work in a extremely isolated context.
- My supervisor doesn't believe in positive feedback. His motto is, ''No news is good news.''
- In eighteen years of teaching in three schools, no supervisor has ever visited my class and thus I have never had another adult give me feedback about my work, pro or con.

I marvel at the resiliency of teachers in these situations. Despite the environment, they usually go about their work in a very professional manner, motivated primarily by the psychic rewards discussed in Chapters 4 and 5.

On the other hand, climates can change quickly. As one teacher put it in a workshop,

> The atmosphere is 100% different than it was last year. Jim's already thanked me three times for something. I never got a thank you in ten years from the other guy.

Certainly it is simplistic to think that all negative school climates can be modified magically by a few TLC comments by a principal. But the fact remains that administrators have a significant impact on climate. In good schools they know that and behave accordingly. All people in the organization are treated with respect and care and are supported in their endeavors. One often finds reports of schools that have been turned around rapidly by new leadership, such as cases portrayed recently in *The Boston Globe* (Kadaba, 1990; Ribadeneira, 1990).

It would be a disservice to administrators to imply that they alone have the responsibility to make their organization a productive and enjoyable place in which to work. All professionals have this responsibility. Unfortunately, based on my observations, there is a small contingent of teachers in too many schools who, even when they are in a good working environment, behave in thoughtless and uncaring ways. They put down students and colleagues, are uncooperative with colleagues and supervisors, are lazy, are disinterested in research, never read a professional journal or book, do not belong to a professional organization, and seldom have a good thing to say about anything. These teachers have a negative impact on climate, and are a drag on the organization's adaptability.

Finally, boards of education have a great impact on climate as well (as do the communities they represent). Their attitudes and behavior send messages that can either boost or undermine morale and motivation. For example, in too many instances a major reason that principals do not supervise their staffs in a systematic way is that their work loads prevent them from doing so. Their already hectic and pressed jobs (as seen in the literature reviewed in previous chapters) are compounded by being responsible for supervising—by themselves—thirty or forty teachers (in addition to other staff such as counselors and special educators). On top of all this, they are responsible for endless lists of other routine tasks ranging from bussing supervision to building maintenance. Compounding many situations is the interference of boards in the management of the school. I know of a case where the board chair signs all purchase orders for expenditures above fifty dollars. In such settings it is nearly impossible to fulfill a quality administrative-leadership role.

It is interesting to note how the private sector has lately paid considerable attention to climate. The book that first highlighted its role was the best-selling *In Search of Excellence* by Peters and Waterman. One of their major themes is that "treating people—not money, machines, or minds—as the natural resource may be the key to it all" (1982, p. 39). Although some reviewers have criticized the book's research methodology and conclusions about factors that are the foundation for an excellent business (Carroll, 1983), the climate theme has been repeated in other business literature (e.g., Kanter, 1983; Waterman, 1987), and thus gained credence as an important "footing for change."

## Psychological Contracts and Organizational Learning

The work climate contributes significantly to the "psychological contract" between employees and their organization.

> The notion of a psychological contract implies that there is an unwritten set of expectations operating at all times between every member of an organization and the various managers and others in that organization. [Schein, 1980, p. 22]

Contracts ebb and flow as employee and organization needs and conditions change; the necessarily dynamic contracts undergo continual renegotiation. The ability of an organization to adapt, to be innovative, and ultimately to do a better job is dependent on the extent to which the system supports and encourages initiative and creative thinking (Schein, 1980, pp. 33-36).

Good schools establish and maintain positive contracts with their employees, thus fostering considerable small-scale change. This was the case with the pattern of innovation uncovered at Bromley and Mansfield. The climates in these schools were instrumental to the psychological contracts prevalent there. Teachers were empowered and motivated to be change agents.

According to Argyris and Schon, "Just as individuals are the agents of organizational action, so they are the agents for organizational learning" (1978, p. 19). Such learning occurs when educators see themselves as representatives of the school with a responsibility to be open to environmental signals that change may be needed, to respond to the signals and consider whether to make adjustments in behavior, and to restructure their learning theory to a new level of effectiveness. Although idealistic, organizational learning becomes a key factor in system adaptability.

Existing evidence about good school climates indicates that they have great potential to become learning organizations. Teachers and administrators in such schools do not just talk about innovation, but effect it—primarily through a small win approach. Over time, these "ordinary" people have the potential to push their organizations to the level of system learning.

## Reflective Practitioners and Adult Learners

Because the school organization contains considerable uncertainty, instability, uniqueness, and value conflict (as seen in Chapter 3), organizational learning is dependent upon professionals who, in their everyday activities, behave spontaneously and intuitively. They possess the qualities of knowing-in-action and even reflection-in-action (Schon, 1983, pp. 21-69).

When individuals who know-in-action confront situations that they perceive as normal, they can make judgments about quality without always being able to state explicit criteria and can apply skills to problem situations without always being able to state the rules and procedures.

When individuals who reflect-in-action confront something out of the ordinary, they realize that old solutions may no longer work. Hence they have to invent alternative solutions or perhaps experiment on the spot to find other solutions.

Although it is often difficult to distinguish clearly between knowing-in-action and reflecting-in-action, the critical point is that well-prepared professionals possess the ability to make the adjustments necessary to meet new situations. Based on the study of Bromley and Mansfield and other related research on good schools where small wins are common, it appears that most educators in such schools are competent problem solvers and that most are close to being reflective practitioners who behave as innovators. If most of them did not behave this way, the organization would not be self-renewing.

During the interviews I conducted, teachers could readily discuss what they had done and why they had done it in dealing with familiar and unfamiliar problem situations. However, they could not describe the spontaneous, intuitive thought processes underlying their actions. ''Like knowing-in-action, reflection-in-action is a process we can deliver without being able to say why we are doing it'' (Schon, 1987, p. 31). Sergiovanni, in applying the ideas of reflective practice to the role of the principal, comes to similar conclusions about this form of knowledge creation and use (1987).

While it may not seem possible in the busy kitchen world of the school to teach employees how to be more reflective in practice, schools can nurture and support this behavior. By doing so, they will promote empowerment and thus use more fully the talents of their staffs.

Good schools treat teachers and other employees as adult learners while recognizing that not everyone is at the same place on the maturity and competence scales. Good schools start with positive assumptions about human nature rather than with turn-of-the-century assumptions that lead them to treat employees as children who need authoritarian administrators to direct and control their behavior (as illustrated by the previously cited comments about supervisor behavior in the ''climate'' section of this chapter). Good schools recognize and value their staffs as the instrumental change agents who deliver relevant and effective education to learners. They see teachers as highly capable, thoughtful individuals who appreciate the support they receive when they do a good job and when they innovate. Good schools treat teachers as professionals rather than as mere technicians plugged into classrooms in order to carry out hierarchical mandates.

In these kinds of schools there is a decided agenda to help teachers become better—and a key to achieving that goal, according to Glickman, is to assist them in developing their ability to think abstractly, which is

the ability to determine relationships, to make comparisons and contrasts between information and experience, and to use these to generate multiple possibilities in formulating a decision. [1990, pp. 60-61]

An abstract thinker and a reflective practitioner share the same definition: an independent change agent who can think and respond to problems rapidly and decisively and who sees being innovative as a major professional responsibility.

However, as Glickman contends, there are numerous factors in the school environment (similar to those described in Chapter 3) that interfere with teachers who aim to become more autonomous people who think abstractly and who identify and solve problems (1990). Therefore, school leaders need to intervene in order to alter those conditions.

Here I will pause to insert a commonplace example of a "factor." I have taught graduate courses for some twenty years. I am continually impressed by the quality of the students I encounter. They are a great potential resource for their schools. Many of them pay for their education and many receive a stipend from their district. After the course is completed, I sometimes ask students, when I see them at a later date, whether their supervisor (who approved the course) asked them to discuss the experience and to share thoughts about how learnings from a fifteen-week investment could be useful locally. Rarely do I hear: "Oh yes, we got together. He was really interested in what I learned, and I'm to submit a list of ideas about next steps." How easy it would be for supervisors to do this—to send an important signal that employees are adult learners who have something to offer to the organization. In turn, the school would benefit by nurturing the development of more "idea champions" (as discussed in Chapter 5).

If school leaders related to their employees in this way, then we would make an impact on one problem that is still all too prevalent in public education—the mindlessness depicted by Silberman in 1970 in *Crisis in the Classroom*. He defined it as "the failure or refusal to think seriously about educational purpose, the reluctance to question established practice" (p. 11). The quotations from students in classes and workshops cited in previous sections of this chapter attest to the continued existence of this sad phenomenon in too many schools. As professionals we have a responsibility to combat mindlessness—not to aid and abet it.

## The Administrator as Teacher

Throughout this book the role of the principal has been highlighted as instrumental to school improvement. However, I have, at the same time, attempted to make clear that this person need not—and indeed should not and cannot—be the person on the fabled white horse leading the charge for virtually all change. The role is too demanding and complex for this to occur. But even if it were not, and the principal could do it in theory, to assume such a role in today's schools would be incompatible with the current movement toward site-based management and shared governance.

Nevertheless, the principal has a significant impact on large- and small-scale innovation, and on overall school improvement. In the portraits of Bromley and Mansfield, the principals were instructional leaders integral to the dynamics of change. They worked hard to support their staffs and to find ways to release the creative energy that is present in most groups of teachers. They were successful at the task and verified a main thesis of Fiedler's approach to understanding leadership — that the most important ingredient for successful leadership is leader-member relations (Fiedler and Chemers, 1984, p. 59). Other noted students of leadership have come to similar conclusions (e.g., Gardner, 1990, pp. 23-37). In addition, the principals recognized the need to individualize, as much as possible, the way that they related to and worked with their staffs [which illustrates, in action, Hersey and Blanchard's concepts about situational leadership (1988)].

These men had worked out an approach to authority, power, and organizational control that led to a productive work environment and productive relationships among employees at all levels, from the custodians, bus drivers, and secretaries to teachers and fellow administrators. Bromley and Mansfield, as is the case for other good schools, had developed positive working conditions, which research is recognizing as central to morale, professional development, and overall effective practice (Louis, 1990).

Finally, I would like to return to a book on management that has made a great impression on me, Levinson's *The Exceptional Executive*. In it the author discusses an exciting metaphor for enriching the life of an administrator — the administrator as teacher, a person who attends to the ministration, maturation, and mastery needs of his employees.

> When the executive views his role as leadership-teaching, the essence of his task is to enhance the capabilities of each of his subordinates and to enable them to strengthen each other toward accomplishing their mutual goals and fulfilling their joint needs. (1968, p. 171)

Gardner advocates for similar attention to this important dimension of leadership when he states, "The consideration leaders must never forget is that the key to renewal is the release of human energy and talent" (1990, p. 136).

As a principal said to me the other day when I was visiting his school, "I have a great staff here. Often I have to put the brakes on them as I'm afraid they'll overdo it." He is well on his way to being an administrator-teacher.

## Perspectives on Time

Organizational climate, psychological contracts, an environment for organizational learning, the role of educator as reflective practitioner and adult learner, and the administrator as teacher all combine to create an organizational perspective on time.

Ringle and Savickas discuss the subjective time orientation of institutions and their employees – i.e., how they view and orient themselves in relation to the past, present, and future (1983, pp. 649-661).

They see these three modalities as having different profiles in different organizations, as represented by Figure 8.2.

While a focus on the past, present, or future may change quickly due to internal or external conditions, most organizations develop a ''preferred'' orientation that affects decision making and innovation.

If the past is dominant, administrators and staff will view themselves as protectors of it who insure that what has worked will continue to steer present and future decisions. ''The institution is a projectile from the past, and the administrator's job is to protect the original trajectory'' (p. 652). Challenges to present practice will often be taken personally and dismissed out of hand.

If the present dominates, the organization may feel rudderless, buffeted about by the latest fads, crises, and daily events.

If the future dominates, there may be such emphasis on what ''should be'' that worthy traditions and lessons from the past are ignored, present opportunities are missed, and employees are seen as idealists disconnected from the ''real world.''

What organizations need to strive for is a balance in perspectives so that there is a healthy mix of remembering the past, experiencing the present, and anticipating the future. From my experience and research, I think that good schools have achieved such a balance and that the perspective on time that permeates organizations such as Bromley and Mansfield contributes in important ways to their ability to adapt.

## CONCLUDING COMMENTS

I have always liked the bumper sticker, ''If you think education is expensive, try ignorance.'' In a simple phrase it captures nicely the reasons why we must improve our schools. We are in the midst of tough economic times, and it will be easy for society to slough off its respon-

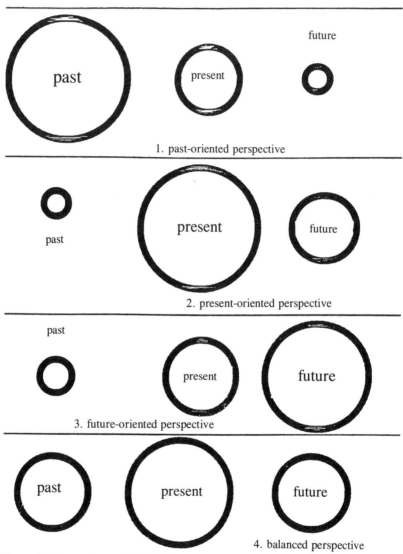

1. past-oriented perspective

2. present-oriented perspective

3. future-oriented perspective

4. balanced perspective

**Figure 8.2** Perspectives on Individual and Organizational Time. Copyright, 1983 by the Ohio State University Press. All rights reserved. Reprinted by permission. Reprinted from Ringle, P. M. and M. L. Savickas. Nov./Dec. 1983. ''Administrative Leadership: Planning and Time Perspective,'' *Journal of Higher Education*, 54(6).

sibilities to public education and for educators to fall into a state of cynicism and despair. That must not happen. Instead, all citizens must reaffirm their commitment to support education and to work hard for its renewal and perhaps even restructuring, for I am not overstating the case when I assert that our survival as a vibrant, humane, and powerful nation depends on the quality of the education provided to our children and youth.

The next decade promises considerable uncertainty for education. This uncertainty is caused partially by the economic situation facing the nation; in most cases, dramatic school improvement requires resources—it is as simple as that. The uncertainty is also caused by the contradictory signals being sent to educators by their various constituencies. Do we respond to the green, red, or yellow sets of expectations? Rather than stopping or proceeding with caution, we must see what is problematic as a challenge and as an opportunity. "In accepting uncertainty, we unlock school reform and enter a new phase of professionalism" (Glickman, 1987, p. 122). By doing so, we will also have great influence over policy makers and communities, a rightful and needed leadership role for administrators, teachers, counselors, special educators, and other personnel.

In the Introduction, I list several themes that permeate this book and demonstrate how they mesh with the cultural perspective on organizations and change. An understanding of these themes will provide another theory of changing to guide action through the 1990s and beyond, as we work to create and recreate the educational system our children need and deserve. To restate them briefly:

- Organizations are always changing but usually in routine, fairly unnoticed ways rather than in dramatic, heroic ways.
- Change is usually effected by ordinary people doing ordinary things competently.
- Routine organizational processes are often key levers for improvement.
- Change occurs in an often unpredictable and not well understood fashion.
- Organizational adaptation is an interplay of rationality and foolishness, of cognition and affect.
- Small wins can set in motion a process for continued small wins—a process that strengthens organizational capacity and ability to solve larger-scale problems.

''Think big, and start small'' should be posted above all our doors. *Changing Schools from the Inside Out* is an effective approach to improvement, an approach that will draw and build on the great engine of energy and inventiveness that exists in all our schools. But there is no magic in it. It is incremental and evolutionary, requiring the support and hard work of all the parties that have an investment in public education in America.

# Appendix

Chapter 4 includes a brief description of the rationale for the study, the conceptual framework, its school selection, and the Bromley and Mansfield schools. This appendix provides more detailed information about the type of study, research design, site selection, data collection, research methods, and data analysis. The field research was conducted while I was on sabbatical leave during the 1981-82 academic year.

## TYPE OF STUDY AND RESEARCH DESIGN

This study falls under the rubric of naturalistic research, as described by Owens (1982, p. 6):

> Thus, if one seeks to understand the realities of human organizations and the behavior of people in them, the naturalistic view would hold that those organizations must be examined in all the rich confusion of their daily existence. Human behavior must be studied *in situ* if it is to be understood.

In this type of inquiry there is direct, ongoing contact between the researcher and the actors in the situation; in this type of inquiry some specifics of the research design may emerge as the study unfolds; in this type of inquiry data categories emerge, most of the time, after rather than before data are collected; and in this type of inquiry no formal "scientific" generalizations are made to a universe beyond the universe of the study itself. Applicability of findings to other situations is the responsibility of the consumer of the research—the reader—with such applicability depending largely on the credibility of the findings and how they are interpreted.

Naturalistic inquiry views the person as a research instrument who must be trained and skilled in using him/herself as the major means of data collection. However, other tools of data collection may be used that will help to understand human behavior and experience from the perspective of the research subject, not the perspective of the investigator.

These tools or methods are usually qualitative rather than quantitative in nature. Thus interviews, observations, documents and records, and questionnaires are primary ways through which to gain an understanding of the thoughts, perceptions, values, feelings, and actions of the research subjects (Owens, pp. 5-8; Lincoln and Guba, 1985, pp. 250-281).

Naturalistic or on-site research may, at the beginning of a study, be ethnographic in nature or much more structured. In the former approach, the investigators "do" ethnography by immersing themselves in the situation, usually for six months to a year or more, drawing on various qualitative methods in order to describe and interpret cultural behavior (Wolcott, 1985). In a more structured approach, four elements — a conceptual framework, research questions, research populations, and instruments for data collection — are identified before the study begins (Miles and Huberman, 1984, pp. 27-48). The roots for such structured inquiry go back to what used to be called "field studies" of organizations,

> . . . attempts to see what is there rather than to predict the relationships that will be found. It represents the earlier stage of a science. From its findings may come knowledge about important relationships between variables. [Katz, 1953, p. 74]

The study of Bromley and Mansfield was structured by the four elements suggested by Miles and Huberman (but my use of them predated their book).

## SITE SELECTION

I wanted to study processes of curricular and instructional change in two medium-sized secondary schools, ones reputed to be "good" schools but not known for being innovative. I also wanted to study schools somewhat removed from the more urban areas of the state, which usually have more money to allocate to school support and which are influenced by a more cosmopolitan, educated local population. I excluded medium-sized schools in ski areas that definitely had higher than average per-pupil costs.

In Vermont, ''medium'' is generally understood to be in the 400-800 students range, in some cases including grades 7-12 and in other cases grades 9-12. Using the criteria of the job stability and reputation of the principals, the school's reputation for quality, existence of up-to-date programs, school compliance with state regulations, and ongoing local support and political stability (e.g., no raging budget battles and community-school conflicts), I asked five veteran educators, familiar with secondary schools statewide, for three selections each. Among the five were two former superintendents who worked at the university in service/field activities with schools statewide, the head of the principals' association, a former deputy commissioner of education, and the state chief of secondary education.

All of the schools were in rural or semi-rural areas. Bromley and Mansfield were top selections, so I talked with the principals individually about the study and the possibility of using their organizations as sites. We then met together so I could explain the project in more detail. They returned to their schools, checked with some teachers about their reactions to the proposal, and gave me permission to go ahead.

## DATA COLLECTION

The fall semester was devoted to on-site research and the spring to data analysis and initial writing.

I spent five total weeks in each organization, early September to mid-October at Bromley and mid-October to early December at Mansfield. I rented a room and lived in each community during the week, which enabled me to attend board meetings, spend time in the community (I was invited to meals at the homes of teachers, administrators, and board members), and then to use the evenings for data analysis and preparation for the next day.

Before arriving on-site, I had obtained information about the schools, their programs, and their staffs. Therefore, I found that I needed to take only two days at the outset to familiarize myself with the overall ''geography'' of the organization and with the specific locations of teacher homerooms, teacher lounges, and department offices.

This large chunk of concentrated time was one factor that enabled me to increase the "trustworthiness" of my findings.

> The basic issue in relation to trustworthiness is simple: How can the inquirer persuade his or her audiences (including self) that the findings of an inquiry are worth paying attention to, worth taking account of? [Lincoln and Guba, 1985, p. 290]

Major ways to increase the "truth value" — the credibility of research outcomes — are to schedule "prolonged engagement" of time on-site, and while there to use "persistent observation." The former promotes scope of activity and the latter promotes depth (pp. 301-305).

Five weeks also allowed me to use several qualitative methods to collect data. Using data from multiple sources — interviews, documents and records, observations, and questionnaires — is "triangulation," a major mode for improving the credibility of findings and interpretations (Lincoln and Guba, 1985, pp. 305-307).

Because the researcher is the major instrument in a naturalistic study, my background as an educator is also a factor in relation to the credibility of outcomes. I taught high school for five years, was an administrator for a year, carried out a year-long dissertation field study in a high school, and have spent twenty-three years in higher education working actively with schools and educators in a service role as well as conducting several research projects in educational organizations. In addition, I was a site visitor and research discussant for the Model Schools Project of the National Association of Secondary School Principals and a site visitor for its Middle Schools Project.

## RESEARCH METHODS

The research methods and data bases are summarized in Table A.1.

### Interviews

A semi-structured interview was designed before the study began and pretested during the summer with six teachers from other schools. It was the primary means of data collection during the first three weeks in the organization. It also served as a major vehicle to enable me to get acquainted with the staffs and to establish rapport and trust.

In many instances it was completed in a forty-five-minute class period, but in most instances I spent an average of 100 minutes with each teacher. Interviews were usually scheduled several days ahead at the convenience of the teacher or staff member (e.g., counselors). Notes were taken openly but no tape recorder was used. Each night I read the notes, a process that helped immensely to give me further insights for subsequent interviews and engaged me in the task of data reduction.

Twelve principal research questions were developed around the Rand framework (described in Chapter 4) of mobilization, implementation, and institutionalization. Some examples of questions are: What were the

*TABLE A.1 The Schools.*

|  | **Bromley** | **Mansfield** |
|---|---|---|
| Average No. of Exploratory Interviews* per person | 98 interviews = 2.4 (avg. 100 min. each) Total N = 41 | 94 interviews = 2.5 (avg. 100 min. each) Total N = 37 |
| Levels of Use Interviews* | 29 interviews | 24 interviews |
| Work Attitudes Interviews* | 18 interviews | 24 interviews |
| Total Interviews | 145 | 142 |
| Stages of Concern Questionnaire | N = 62 | N = 49 |
| Work Attitudes Questionnaire | N = 33 | N = 28 |
| Board Minutes 75-81 | Examined | Examined |
| Program of Studies and Related Materials | Examined | Examined |

*Interviews @ 40 minutes each.

sources of the innovation and why was it adopted or developed? Who played what roles? What processes were involved in implementing the innovation? What caused an innovation to be dropped?

No teacher refused to be interviewed. There were only three times when someone scheduled to be interviewed forgot the appointment, but in each case another time was found. There were only two occasions when a teacher said, "Don't write this down."

In order to maximize use of time when it was not possible to fill a period with a teacher interview, I often was able to schedule "pop in" sessions with individuals whose schedules were more flexible. The principal, assistant principal, and counselors were very cooperative in responding to these sudden requests for their time.

In total, I spent about twelve hours of interview time with each principal (using a different set of questions). I also interviewed the superintendent and the board chairs.

Primarily during the last two weeks in each school, I also used a shorter interview with selected teachers about the nature of teaching as work. I picked the sample on the basis of the initial interview where I made assessments about which people could contribute the most to this set of questions. They were based on Dan Lortie's classic study of the profession (1975) and focused on teacher tasks, feelings about teaching, motivators, and job satisfiers.

The validated Levels of Use interview (LoU – see Chapter 6) was the third interview conducted with selected teachers (see Hall and Hord, 1987, for a full description of the Concerns-Based Adoption Model from which it is drawn. See also Hord, S. M. et al.). Initially, several were taped so I could do a "reliability check" on myself in terms of using the structured process. During the summer, under the guidance of Beulah Newlove, a project associate of Gene Hall's at the then-Research and Development Center for Teacher Education at the University of Texas at Austin, I conducted test interviews to become a certified LoU interviewer. Such certification was necessary to increase the validity of interview results. Interviews, for a class period, were conducted with teachers who, based on the initial interview, were involved in a substantive way with an innovation appropriate for the application of LoU methodology.

Incorporated into the LoU interview was an open-ended statement to surface concerns about the innovation. Interviewees were asked, "When you think about the innovation, what are you concerned about?"

## Questionnaires

Further inquiry about concerns was conducted through the Stages of Concern Questionnaire, which was used in conjunction with the two mandated innovations – staffings and basic competencies – described in Chapter 6. The instruments were given to teachers involved with these innovations. They were returned at rates of 86 percent and 82 percent, and processed by Gene Hall's office.

To insure a high rate of cooperation, these were not disseminated until the fourth week in the schools when I had completed the initial interviews. By then, I had established a good working relationship with the staff. That relationship paid off right after I had put some questionnaires in mailboxes. Within a few hours, three teachers sought me out to tell me that they didn't understand the cover sheet. Fortunately, I retrieved most of the instruments and rewrote the instructions. Another time around I would seek such feedback first.

I used one other paper and pencil device near the end of the period in each organization. It was a validated, twenty-three item "Sense of Autonomy" questionnaire (Packard et al., 1973). These were completed at rates of 80 percent and 70 percent. It was an illustration of an "emergent strategy." When I began the study I did not foresee the need for such an instrument. However, near the completion of the initial interviews, at Bromley, I realized that some means to assess feelings of teacher autonomy would be very useful to the research. I remembered such an instrument from my previous sabbatical leave at the University of Oregon. Thus began a series of calls to track it down.

## Documents and Records

The major documents analyzed were school board minutes, programs of study, and miscellaneous circular materials. I listened to several staffings tapes at Bromley. Documents and records served the very useful purpose of "filling" unscheduled time in my interview schedule. Many hours on-site were devoted to this activity.

## Observation

Systematic, detailed participant observation was not necessary, given the purposes of the study. However, five weeks in each organization enabled me to engage in the "persistent observation" recommended by Lincoln and Guba. It served the purpose ". . . to identify those characteristics and elements in the situation that are most relevant to the problem or issue being pursued and focusing on them in detail" (p. 304).

Observations took place primarily in the formal settings of faculty and school board meetings and basic staffing sessions for Public Law 94-142. Informal observation took place in department offices, the teachers' lounges, the main office, the corridors, the lunchroom, and in a few classrooms.

Being "out and around" was valuable for another important reason. Encountering people during the course of daily activities sometimes prompted spontaneous comments that gave me a reading about my relationship to some individuals or how I was being accepted by the organization. For example, in the teachers' lounge a teacher said, "I hope I'm being helpful. There are times I'm concerned that I'm not giving you the information you are looking for." Or a counselor said at lunch, "Things seem to be going well for you. I've heard several people say that you seem to be one of the faculty and that they really enjoy sitting down and talking with you." Sometimes, while passing in the corridor, I would hear, "Do we have an appointment today or tomorrow?" And, after being absent from a faculty meeting, a teacher said, "Where were you today? You missed a classic case of the principal blowing it."

Being on-site also enabled me to engage in "member checks," the process of seeking feedback about tentative findings and interpretation or getting answers to questions from stakeholding groups (Lincoln and Guba, 1985, pp. 314-316). This technique is another way to increase the credibility of outcomes.

## Data Analysis

As indicated earlier, data analysis was a continuous iterative process as recommended by Bogdan and Biklen (1982, pp. 146-155) and Miles and Huberman (1984, pp. 21-23). Being on-site for five weeks and living in the communities provided me with time each evening to sort through and examine data collected that day. The process promoted the reduction of data, which involves focusing, simplifying, abstracting, and transforming it.

In any naturalistic study, wrestling with the inevitable "five drawers of field notes" can, at first, be an overwhelming task. Initially, I found the qualitative data (to use Miles' term) "an attractive nuisance" (1979), but working with it daily on-site proved to be a wise step. Therefore, once the field research was completed, I was able to begin more quickly coding data—placing it into working catetories so that it could be organized into regularities, patterns, and themes. While engaged in this analysis, I sometimes "member-checked" by phone with the principal or staff.

Following the advice of Miles and Huberman, I strove to count data, whenever it seemed sensible to do so, so that it could be put into tabular form. Other data I tried to place in some kind of display such as a figure or chart that would move it into a shape beyond pure narrative text, which is typical of studies relying on qualitative methodology.

# Bibliography

Addison Northeast Supervisory Union. 1989. *School Report* 1989. Bristol, VT.

American Association of School Administrators. 1988. *School-Based Management.* Arlington, VA.

Argyris, C. and D. A. Schön. 1978. *Organizational Learning: A Theory in Action Perspective.* Reading, MA: Addison-Wesley Publishing Co.

Ashton, P. T. and R. B. Webb. 1986. *Making a Difference: Teachers' Sense of Efficacy.* New York, NY: Longman.

Barnett, H. G. 1953. Innovation: *The Basis of Cultural Change.* New York, NY: McGraw-Hill Book Company.

Bell, D. 1973. *The Coming of Post-Industrial Society.* New York, NY: Basic Books.

Benne, K. D., W. G. Bennis, and R. Chin. 1976. "Planned Change in America," in *The Planning of Change* (3rd ed.). W. G. Bennis, K. D. Benne, and R. Chin, eds. New York, NY: Holt, Rinehart, & Winston, pp. 13-45.

Bentzen, M.M. and Associates. 1974. *Changing Schools: The Magic Feather Principle.* New York, NY: McGraw-Hill Book Company.

Berliner, D. C. 1984. "The Half-Full Glass: A Review of Research on Teaching," in *Using What We Know about Teaching.* P. L. Hosford, ed. Alexandria, VA: Association for Supervision and Curriculum Development, pp. 51-84.

Berman, P. 1981. "Educational Change: An Implementation Paradigm," in *Improving Schools: Using What We Know,* R. Lehming, and M. Kane, eds. Beverly Hills, CA: Sage Publications, pp. 253-286.

Berman, P. and M. W. McLaughlin. 1978. *Federal Programs Supporting Educational Change, Vol. VIII: Implementing and Sustaining Innovations.* Santa Monica, CA: The Rand Corporation.

Bloom, B. S. 1980. "The New Direction in Education Research: Alterable Variables," *Phi Delta Kappan,* 61(6):382-385.

Bogdan, R. C. and S. K. Biklen. 1982. *Qualitative Research for Education.* Boston: Allyn and Bacon.

Bossert, S. T., D. C. Dwyer, B. Rowen, and G. Y. Lee. 1982. "The Instructional Management Role of the Principal," *Educational Administration Quarterly,* 28(3):34-64.

141

*The Boston Globe.* 1989. "State Board Seizes Control of Schools in Jersey City" (October 5):3.

Botsford, K. 1989. "Assignment: Chelsea Schools," *Bostonia*, 63(6):33-41.

Boyer, E. L. 1983. *High School: A Report on Secondary Education in America.* New York, NY: Harper and Row.

Bradley, A. 1990. "In Rochester, Skepticism, Confusion Greet News of'Revolutionary' Pact," *Education Week*, 10(4):1, 13.

*The Burlington Free Press.* 1991. "Education Aid Likely to Decline"(January 16): 2B.

Carlson, R. V. and G. Awkerman, eds. 1991. *Educational Planning: Concepts, Strategies, Practices.* New York, NY: Longman.

Carnegie Forum on Education and the Economy. 1986. *A Nation Prepared: Teachers for the 21st Century.* New York, NY: Carnegie Corporation.

Carnegie Foundation for the Advancement of Teaching. 1988. *Teacher Involvement in Decision Making: A State-by-State Profile.* New York, NY: Carnegie Corporation.

Carroll, D. T. 1983. "A Disappointing Search for Excellence," *Harvard Business Review*, 61(6):78-79, 82-83.

Carroll, J. M. 1990. "The Copernican Plan: Restructuring the American High School," *Phi Delta Kappan*, 71(5):358-365.

Cetron, M. J. 1988. "Class of 2000: The Good News and the Bad News," *The Futurist*, 22(6):9-15.

Christensen, S. 1979. "Decision Making and Socialization," in *Ambiguity and Choice in Organizations*, Second Edition. J. G. March and J. P. Olsen, eds. Bergen, Norway: Universitetsforlaget, pp. 351-396.

Clark, D. L. and S. McKibbin. 1982. "From Orthodoxy to Pluralism: New Views of School Administration," *Phi Delta Kappan*, 63(10):669-672.

Clune, W. H. and P. A. White. 1988. *School-Based Management.* New Brunswick, NJ: Rutgers, The State University of New Jersey, Center for Policy Research in Education.

Cohen, M. 1989. "Bennett Says U.S. Governors Agree on Keeping Drugs Out of Schools," *The Boston Globe*, (September 28):18.

Cohen, M. D., J. G. March, and J. P. Olsen. 1972. "A Garbage Can Model of Organizational Choice," *Administrative Science Quarterly*, 17(1):1-25.

Cohen, M. D., J. G. March, and J. P. Olsen. 1979. "People, Problems, Solutions, and the Ambiguity of Relevance," in *Ambiguity and Choice in Organizations*, Second Edition. J. G. March and J. P. Olsen, eds. Bergen, Norway: Universitetsforlaget, pp. 24-37.

Conant, J. B. 1959. *The American High School Today.* New York, NY: McGraw-Hill Book Company.

Conant, J. B. 1969. *The Comprehensive High School.* New York, NY: McGraw-Hill Book Company.

Cook, B. 1990. *Strategic Planning for America's Schools*, Second Edition. Arlington, VA: American Association of School Administrators.

Corbett, H. D. 1982. "Principals' Contributions to Maintaining Change," *Phi Delta Kappan*, 64(3):190-192.

Cornish, E. 1990. "Issues of the '90s," *The Futurist*, 24(1):29-36.

Council on Adolescent Development. 1989. *Turning Points: Preparing American Youth for the 21st Century.* Washington, D.C.

Cuban, L. 1982. "Persistent Instruction: The High School Classroom, 1900-1980," *Phi Delta Kappan*, 64(2):113-118.

Cuban, L. 1984. *How Teachers Taught: Constancy and Change in American Classrooms, 1890-1980.* New York, NY: Longman.

Cuban, L. 1986. "Persistent Instruction: Another Look at Constancy in the Classroom," *Phi Delta Kappan*, 68(1):7-11.

Cuban, L. 1988. "A Fundamental Puzzle of School Reform," *Phi Delta Kappan*, 69(5):341-344.

Cuban, L. 1988. "Why Do Some Reforms Persist?" *Educational Administration Quarterly*, 24(3):329-335.

Cuban, L. 1990. "What I Learned from What I Had Forgotten about Teaching: Notes from a Professor," *Phi Delta Kappan*, 71(6):479-482.

Daft, R. L. and S. W. Becker. 1978. *Innovation in Organizations: Innovation Adoption in School Organizations.* New York, NY: Elsevier.

David, J. L. 1989. "Synthesis of Research on School-based Management," *Educational Leadership*, 46(8):45-53.

Du Four, R. and R. Eaker. 1987. *Fulfilling the Promise of Excellence: A Practitioner's Guide to School Improvement.* Westbury, NY: J. L. Wilkerson Publishing Company.

Dwyer, D. C., G. V. Lee, B. Rowan, and S. T. Bossert. 1983. *Five Principals in Action: Perspectives on Instructional Management.* San Francisco, CA: Far West Laboratory for Educational Research and Development.

*Educational Leadership.* 1983. 41(3):3-36.

Elam, S. 1989. *Prototype: An Anthology of School Improvement Ideas That Work.* Bloomington, IN: Phi Delta Kappa.

Elmore, R. F. and M. W. McLaughlin. 1988. *Steady Work: Policy, Practice, and the Reform of American Education.* Santa Monica, CA: The Rand Corporation.

English, F. W. 1987. *Curriculum Management for Schools—Colleges—Business.* Springfield, IL: Charles C. Thomas Publisher.

English, F. W. 1988. *Curriculum Auditing.* Lancaster, PA: Technomic Publishing Company Inc.

Etzioni, A. 1989. "Humble Decision Making," *Harvard Business Review*, 89(4):122-126.

Fiedler, F. E. and M. M. Chemers. 1984. *Improving Leadership Effectiveness: The Leader Match Concept*, Second Edition. New York, NY: John Wiley & Sons, Inc.

Franklin, M. C. 1991. "An Old Problem Gets Worse: Teacher Isolation," *The Boston Globe* (February 3):A25-26.

Freed, C. W. and M. E. Ketchem. 1986. "Teacher Paperwork Study: Type, Time, and Difficulty," Dover, DE: Department of Public Instruction.

Fullan, M. 1982. *The Meaning of Educational Change.* New York, NY: Columbia University, Teachers College Press.

Fullan, M. and A. Pomfret. 1977. "Research on Curriculum and Instruction Implementation," *Review of Educational Research*, 47(1):335-397.

Futrell, M. H. 1989. "Mission Not Accomplished: Education Reform in Retrospect," *Phi Delta Kappan*, 71(1):9-14.

Gardner, J. W. 1990. *On Leadership*. New York, NY: The Free Press.

Geggis, A. 1990. "Schools Lack Bucks for Books," *The Burlington Free Press* (July 1):1B.

General Assembly of the State of Vermont. 1990. "No. 230. An Act Relating to Reforms in Special Education."

Georgiou, P. 1973. "The Goal Paradigm and Notes Toward a Counter Paradigm," *Administrative Science Quarterly*, 18(3):291-310.

Glickman, C. D. 1987. "Unlocking School Reform: Uncertainty as a Condition of Professionalism," *Phi Delta Kappan*, 69(2):120-122.

Glickman, C. D. 1990. *Supervision of Instruction: A Developmental Approach*, Second Edition. Boston, MA: Allyn & Bacon.

Glickman, C. D. 1990. "Pushing School Reform to the Edge: The Seven Ironies of School Empowerment," *Phi Delta Kappan*, 72(1):68-75.

Goodlad, J. I. 1984. *A Place Called School*. New York, NY: McGraw-Hill Book Company.

Gottfredson, G. D. and L. G. Hybl. 1987. *An Analytical Description of the School Principal's Job*. Baltimore, MD: The Johns Hopkins University, Center for Research on Elementary and Middle Schools.

Guskey, T. R. 1990. "Integrating Innovations," *Educational Leadership*, 47(5):11-15.

Hall, G. E., A. A. George, and W. L. Rutherford. 1979. *Measuring Stages of Concern about the Innovation: A Manual for Use of the SoC Questionnaire*. Austin, TX: The University of Texas, Research and Development Center for Teacher Education.

Hall, G. E. and S. M. Hord. 1987. *Change in Schools: Facilitating the Process*. Albany, NY: SUNY Press.

Hall, G. E. and W. L. Rutherford. 1990. "Stages of Concern," paper presented at the Annual Meeting of the American Education Research Association, Boston, MA.

Harp, L. 1991. "States' Fiscal Woes Put Education on the Defensive," *Education Week*, 10(18):22-25.

Herriott, R. E. and N. Gross, eds. 1979. *The Dynamics of Planned Educational Change*. Berkeley, CA: McCutchan Publishing Corporation.

Hersey, P. and K. H. Blanchard. 1988. *Management of Organizational Behavior*, Fifth Edition. Englewood Cliffs, NJ: Prentice Hall.

*Horace*. 1989. "The Coalition of Essential Schools," 5(4). Providence, RI: Brown University.

*Horace*. 1990. "The Coalition of Essential Schools," 7(2). Providence, RI: Brown University.

Hord, S. M., Senior Research Associate, Southwest Educational Development Laboratory, 211 E. Seventh St., Austin, TX 78701, can be contacted for information about Concerns-Based Adoption Model (CBAM) research instruments.

Hord, S. M. 1991. Personal Communication.

Hord, S. M., W. L. Rutherford, L. Huling-Austin, and G. E. Hall. 1987. *Taking Charge of Change*. Alexandria, VA: Association for Supervision and Curriculum Development.

House, E. R. 1981. "Three Perspectives on Innovation," in *Improving Schools: Using What We Know*. R. Lehming and M. Kane, eds. Beverly Hills, CA: SAGE Publications, pp. 17-41.

Howard, E., B. Howell, and E. Brainard. 1987. *Handbook for Conducting School Climate Improvement Projects*. Bloomington, IN: Phi Delta Kappa.

Huberman, A. M. and M. P. Miles. 1984. *Innovation Up Close*. New York, NY: Plenum Press.

Huberman, M. 1983. "Recipes for Busy Kitchens," *Knowledge: Creation, Diffusion, Utilization*, 4(4):478-511.

Jackson, P. W. 1968. *Life in Classrooms*. Chicago, IL: Holt, Rinehart, & Winston, Inc.

Johnson, L. B. 1965. "Message to Congress on Education," *The New York Times* (January 26):20.

Kadaba, L. S. 1990. "3 Heroes at the Helm: Holland Is Praised for Rescuing School," *The Boston Globe* (July 8):39-40.

Kanter, R. M. 1983. *The Change Masters*. New York, NY: Simon & Shuster.

Katz, D. 1953. "Field Studies," in *Research Methods in the Behavioral Sciences*, L. Festinger and D. Katz, eds. New York: Holt, Rinehart & Winston.

Katz, D. and R. L. Kahn. 1978. *The Social Psychology of Organizations*, Second Edition. New York, NY: John Wiley & Sons, Inc.

Kaufman, R. and J. Herman. 1991. *Strategic Planning in Education: Rethinking, Restructuring, Revitalizing*. Lancaster, PA: Technomic Publishing Company, Inc.

Kelley, E. A. 1980. *Improving School Climate*. Reston, VA: National Association of Secondary School Principals.

Kirst, M.K. 1982. "How to Improve Schools Without Spending More Money," *Phi Delta Kappan*, 64(1):6-8.

Kottkamp, R. B., E. F. Provenzo, and M.M. Cohn. 1986. "Stability and Change in a Profession: Two Decades of Teacher Attitudes, 1964-1984," *Phi Delta Kappan*, 67(8):559-567.

Kouzes, J. M. and B. Z. Posner. 1987. *The Leadership Challenge*. San Francisco, CA: Jossey-Bass.

Larson, R. L. 1982. "Planning in Garbage Cans: Notes from the Field," *The Journal of Educational Administration*, 20(2):47-60.

Larson, R. L. 1988. "Change Process" and "Change Variables," in *Encyclopedia of School Administration and Supervision*. R. A. Gorton, G. T. Schneider, and J. C. Fisher, eds. Phoenix, AZ: Oryx Press, pp. 52-55.

Larson, R. L. 1991. "Small Is Beautiful: Innovation from the Inside Out," *Phi Delta Kappan*, 72(7):550-554.

Levinson, H. 1968. *The Exceptional Executive: A Psychological Conception*. New York, NY: New American Library.

Lewis, A. 1989. *Restructuring America's Schools*. Arlington, VA: American Association of School Administrators.

Lieberman, A. and L. Miller. 1984. *Teachers, Their World, and Their Work*. Alexandria, VA: Association for Supervision and Curriculum Development.

Lightfoot, S. L. 1983. *The Good High School*. New York, NY: Basic Books, Inc.

Lincoln, Y. S. and E. G. Guba. 1985. *Naturalistic Inquiry*. Beverly Hills: SAGE Publications.

Lipsitz, J. 1984. *Successful Schools for Young Adolescents.* New Brunswick, NJ: Transaction Books.

Lortie, D.C. 1969. "The Balance of Control and Autonomy in Elementary School Teaching," in *The Semi-Professions and Their Organization.* A. Etzioni, ed. New York, NY: The Free Press, pp. 1-53.

Lortie, D. C. 1975. *Schoolteacher: A Sociological Study.* Chicago, IL: The University of Chicago Press.

Loucks, S. F., B. W. Newlove, and G. E. Hall. 1975. *Measuring Levels of Use of the Innovation: A Manual for Trainers, Interviewers, and Raters.* Austin, TX: The University of Texas, Research and Development Center for Teacher Education.

Loucks, S. F. and D. A. Zacchei. 1983. "Applying Our Findings to Today's Innovations," *Educational Leadership,* 41(3):28-31.

Loucks-Horsley, S. and L. F. Hergert. 1985. *An Action Guide to School Improvement.* Alexandria, VA: Association for Supervision and Curriculum Development.

Louis, K. S. and M. B. Miles. 1990. *Improving the Urban High School: What Works and Why.* New York, NY: Columbia University, Teachers College Press.

Maeroff, G. I. 1988. *The Empowerment of Teachers.* New York, NY: Columbia University, Teachers College Press.

Manasse, A. L. 1985. "Improving Conditions for Principal Effectiveness: Policy Implications of Research," *The Elementary School Journal,* 85(3):439-463.

March, J. G. 1981. "Footnotes to Organizational Change," *Administrative Science Quarterly,* 26:563-577.

March, J. G. 1983. "How We Talk and How We Act: Administrative Theory and Administrative Life," in *Leadership and Organizational Culture: New Perspectives on Administrative Theory and Practice.* T. Sergiovanni and J. J. Corbally, eds. Urbana, IL: University of Illinois Press, pp. 18-35.

March, J. G. and J. P. Olsen. 1986. "Garbage Can Models of Decision Making in Organizations," in *Ambiguity and Command: Organizational Perspectives on Military Decision Making.* J. G. March and R. Weissinger-Baylon, eds. Cambridge, MA: Harvard Business School Press, pp. 11-35.

Martin, W. J. and D. T. Willower. 1981. "The Managerial Behavior of High School Principals," *Educational Administration Quarterly,* 17(1):69-90.

Mathis, M. 1989. "In Finance Arena, a New Activism Emerges," *Education Week,* 8(31):1, 8, 10.

McAvoy, B. 1987. "Everyday Acts: How Principals Influence Development of Their Staffs," *Educational Leadership,* 44(5):73-77.

McCune, S. D. 1986. *Guide to Strategic Planning for Educators.* Alexandria, VA: Association for Supervision and Curriculum Development.

McDonnell, L. M. and R. F. Elmore. 1987. "Getting the Job Done: Alternative Policy Instruments," *Evaluation and Policy Analysis,* 9(2):133-152.

Miles, M. B., ed. 1964. *Innovation in Education.* New York, NY: Columbia University Teachers College Press.

Miles, M. B. 1973. "Planned Change and Organizational Health: Figure and Ground," in *Educational Administration and the Behavioral Sciences: A Systems Perspective.* M. M. Milstein and J. A. Belasko, eds. Boston, MA: Allyn & Bacon, pp. 429-456.

Miles, M. B. 1979. "Qualitative Data as an Attractive Nuisance," *Administrative Science Quarterly,* 24:590-601.

Miles, M. B. 1980. "School Innovation from the Ground Up: Some Dilemmas," *New York University Education Quarterly,* 11(2):2-9.

Miles, M. B. 1981. "Mapping the Common Properties of Schools," in *Improving Schools: Using What We Know.* R. Lehming, and M. Kane, eds. Beverly Hills, CA: SAGE Publications, pp. 42-114.

Miles, M. B. 1983. "Unraveling the Mystery of Institutionalization," *Educational Leadership,* 41(3):14-19.

Miles, M. B. and A. M. Huberman. 1984. *Qualitative Data Analysis: A Sourcebook of New Methods.* Beverly Hills, CA: SAGE Publications.

Naisbitt, J. 1982. *Megatrends.* New York, NY: Warner Books.

Naisbitt, J. and P. Aburdene. 1990. *Megatrends 2000: Ten New Directions for the 1990's.* New York, NY: William Morrow & Company, Inc.

*NASSP Bulletin.* 1977. 61(412):entire issue.

National Commission on Excellence in Education. 1983. *A Nation at Risk: The Imperative for Educational Reform.* Washington, D.C.: U.S. Government Printing Office.

National Council of Teachers of Mathematics. 1989. *Curriculum and Evaluation Standards for School Mathematics.* Reston, VA.

National Diffusion Network. 1990. *Educational Programs That Work,* Sixteenth Edition. Longmont, CO: Sophis West Inc.

National Governors' Association. 1986. *The Governors' 1991 Report on Education.* Washington, D.C.

National Governors' Association. 1990. "National Goals Statement," *Education Week,* 9(24):16-17.

*NEA Today.* 1990. "Back to School Means Starting Over," 9(1):4-5.

*NEA Today.* 1990. "Kentucky Overhauls Its Schools," 9(2):4-5.

Olson, L. 1990. "N.G.A. Lists Strategies for Achieving National Goals," *Education Week,* 9(40):7.

Olson, L. 1990. "One Year after Takeover by State, Cautious Optimism in Jersey City," *Education Week,* 10(5):1, 20-21.

Olson, L. and J. A. Miller. 1991. "The Education President at Midterm: Mismatch Between Rhetoric, Results?" *Education Week,* 10(16):1, 30, 31.

Orlosky, D. and B. O. Smith. 1972. "Educational Change: Its Origins and Characteristics," *Phi Delta Kappan,* 53(7):412-414.

Osborne, D. 1991. "Governing in the 90's: How Governor William Weld Intends to 'Reinvent' State Government," *The Boston Globe* (January 13):65, 68.

Owens, R. G. 1982. "Methodological Rigor in Naturalistic Inquiry," *Educational Administration Quarterly,* 18(2):1-21.

Packard, J. S., R. O. Carlson, W. W. Charters, Jr., R. A. Moser, and P. A. Schmuck. 1976. *Governance and Task Interdependence in Schools: Final Report of a Longitudinal Study.* Eugene, OR: University of Oregon, Center for Educational Policy and Management.

Passow, A. H. 1989. "Present and Future Directions in School Reform," in *Schooling for Tomorrow.* T. J. Sergiovanni and J. H. Moore, eds. Boston, MA: Allyn & Bacon, pp. 13-39.

Peck, J. 1984. "Kaagan Tags New Standards at $16 Million," *The Burlington Free Press* (February 17):1B, 4B.

Pellegrin, R. J. 1976. "Schools as Work Organizations," in *Handbook of Work,*

*Organization, and Society*. R. Dubin, ed. Chicago, IL: Rand McNally & Company, pp. 343-374.

Pellicer, L. L., L. N. Anderson, J. W. Keefe, E. A. Kelley, and L. E. McCleary. 1988. *High School Leaders and Their Schools – Volume I*. Reston, VA: National Association of Secondary School Principals.

Pellicer, L. L., L. N. Anderson, J. W. Keefe, E. A. Kelley, and L. E. McCleary. 1990. *High School Leaders and Their Schools – Volume II*. Reston, VA: National Association of Secondary School Principals.

Peters, T. J. and R. H. Waterman. 1982. *In Search of Excellence: Lessons from America's Best Run Companies*. New York, NY: Harper and Row.

Pitsch, M. 1990. "Cavazos Creates Outreach Office to Promote Choice," *Education Week,* 10(15):30.

Pitsch, M. 1991. "Bush Seeks to Reward District Plans That Include Private-School Choice," *Education Week,* 10(21):1, 29.

Powell, A. G., E. Farrar, and D. K. Cohen. 1985. *The Shopping Mall High School: Winners and Losers in the Educational Marketplace*. Boston, MA: Houghton Mifflin Company.

Powell, M. 1984. "VT Schools Learn Reform Is Costly," *The Burlington Free Press* (September 4):1A.

Purkey, S. C., R. A. Rutter, and F. M. Newmann. 1986. "U.S. High School Improvement Programs: A Profile from the High School and Beyond Supplemental Survey," *Metropolitan Education*, 3:59-91.

Rasky, S. F. 1990. "Substantial Power on Spending Is Shifted from Congress to Bush," *The New York Times* (October 30):1, 22.

Rauth, M. 1990. "Exploring Heresy in Collective Bargaining with School Restructuring," *Phi Delta Kappan,* 71(10):781-784.

Ravitch, D. 1983. *The Troubled Crusade: American Education, 1945-1980*. New York, NY: Basic Books.

Ribadeneira, D. 1990. "Springfield School Chief Is Turning Tide, Heads," *The Boston Globe* (September 4):25-26.

Ringle, P. M. and M. L. Savickas. 1983. "Administrative Leadership: Planning and Time Perspectives," *Journal of Higher Education*, 54(6):649-661.

Rogers, E. M. 1983. *Diffusion of Innovations*, Third Edition. New York, NY: The Free Press.

Rogers, E. M. and R. A. Rogers. 1976. *Communication in Organizations*. New York, NY: The Free Press.

Ross, D., ed. 1958. *Administration for Adaptability*. New York, NY: Metropolitan School Study Council.

Rutherford, W. L. and L. Huling-Austin. 1984. "Changes in High Schools: What Is Happening – What Is Wanted," paper presented at the annual meeting of the American Educational Research Association, New Orleans, LA.

Sarason, S. B. 1982. *The Culture of the School and the Problem of Change*, Second Edition. Boston, MA: Allyn & Bacon.

Sarason, S. B. 1983. *Schooling in America: Scapegoat and Salvation*. New York, NY: The Free Press.

Sarason, S. B. 1990. *The Coming Failure of Education Reform*. San Francisco, CA: Jossey-Bass.

Schein, E. H. 1980. *Organizational Psychology*, Third Edition. Englewood Cliffs, NJ: Prentice-Hall.

Schön, D. A. 1983. *The Reflective Practitioner*. New York, NY: Basic Books.

Schön, D. A. 1987. *Educating the Reflective Practitioner*. San Francisco, CA: Jossey-Bass.

Sergiovanni, T. J. 1987. *The Principalship: A Reflective Practice Perspective*. Boston: Allyn & Bacon.

Sieber, S. D. 1981. "Knowledge Utilization in Public Education: Incentives and Disincentives," in *Improving Schools: Using What We Know*. R. Lehming and M. Kane, eds. Beverly Hills, CA: SAGE Publications, pp. 115-167.

Silberman, C. 1970. *Crisis in the Classroom*. New York, NY: Random House.

Sirkin, J. R. 1985. "Experts Predict Struggle Ahead to Maintain Education Funding," *Education Week*, 4(31):6.

Sizer, T. R. 1984. *Horace's Compromise: The Dilemma of the American High School*. Boston, MA: Houghton Mifflin Company.

Smith, L. M., D. C. Dwyer, J. J. Prunty, and P. F. Kleine. 1988. *Innovation and Change in Schooling: History, Politics, and Agency*. New York, NY: The Falmer Press.

Smith, L. M., J. J. Prunty, D. C. Dwyer, and P. F. Kleine. 1988. *The Fate of an Innovative School*. New York, NY: The Falmer Press.

Smith, L. M., P. F. Kleine, J. J. Prunty, and D. C. Dwyer. 1986. *Educational Innovators: Then and Now*. New York, NY: The Falmer Press.

Snider, W. 1990. "Parents as Partners," *Education Week*, 10(12):11-17.

South Burlington School District. 1988. *Staff Development Program: 1988-1991*. South Burlington, VT.

Steffy, B. E. 1989. *Curriculum Reform in Kentucky: A Rationale and Proposal*. Frankfort, KY: Department of Education.

Timar, T. 1989. "The Politics of School Restructuring," *Phi Delta Kappan*, 71(4):265-275.

Timar, T. B. and D. L. Kirp. 1989. "Educational Reform in the 1980s: Lessons from the States," *Phi Delta Kappan*, 70(7):504-511.

Toch, T. 1983. "Longer Year, Higher Pay to Be Costly, Study Says," *Education Week*, 3(6):1, 19.

Toffler, A. 1971. *Future Shock*. New York, NY: Bantam Books.

Toffler, A. 1981. *The Third Wave*. New York, NY: Bantam Books.

Toffler, A. 1990. *Powershift*. New York, NY: Bantam Books.

Trump, J. L. 1959. *Images of the Future*. Washington, D.C.: National Association of Secondary School Principals.

Trump, J. L. 1977. *A School for Everyone*. Reston, VA: National Association of Secondary School Principals.

Trump, J. L. and D. Baynham. 1961. *Focus on Change: Guide to Better Schools*. Chicago, IL: Rand McNally & Company.

Trump, J. L. and W. Georgiades. 1970. "Doing Better with What You Have," *The Bulletin of the National Association of Secondary School Principals*, 54(346):106-133.

Trump, J. L. and W. Georgiades. 1977. "What Happened and What Did Not Happen in the Model Schools," *The Bulletin* of the National Association of Secondary School Principals, 61(409):72-79.

Tuthill, D. 1990. "Expanding the Union Contract: One Teacher's Perspective," *Phi Delta Kappan*, 71(10):775-780.

Tyack, D. 1990. " 'Restructuring' in Historical Perspective: Tinkering Toward Utopia," *Teachers College Record*, 92(2):170-191.

Tye, L. 1990. "Downturn Forces Deficits in 30 States," *The Boston Globe* (November 23):1, 38-40.

Tye, K. A. and B. B. Tye. 1984. "Teacher Isolation and School Reform," *Phi Delta Kappan*, 65(5):319-322.

*U.S. News and World Report*. 1990. "Blackboard Jungle" (December 24):52-56.

*U.S. News and World Report*. 1988. "A Blueprint for Better Schools" (January 18):60-65.

*U.S. News and World Report*. 1989. "The Hard Lessons of School Reform" (June 26): 58-60.

*U.S. News and World Report*. 1988. "School Reform, School Reality" (June 20): 58-63.

Vickery, T. R. 1988. "Learning from an Outcomes Driven School District," *Educational Leadership*, 45(5):52-56.

Vickery, T. R. 1990. "ODDM: A Workable Model for Total School Improvement," *Educational Leadership*, 47(7):67-70.

Walker, R. 1990. "Lawmakers in Kentucky Approve Landmark School-Reform Bill," *Education Week*, 6(28):1, 34-35.

Waller, W. 1965. *The Sociology of Teaching*. New York, NY: John Wiley & Sons, Inc.

Waterman, R. H., Jr. 1987. *The Renewal Factor*. New York, NY: Bantam Books.

Watts, G. D. and R. M. McClure. 1990. "Expanding the Contract to Revolutionize School Renewal," *Phi Delta Kappan*, 71(10):765-774.

Weick, K. E. 1976. "Educational Organizations as Loosely Coupled Systems," *Administrative Science Quarterly*, 21:1-19.

Weick, K. E. 1982. "Management of Organizational Change Among Loosely Coupled Elements," in *Change in Organizations: New Perspectives on Theory, Research, and Practice*. P. S. Goodman & Associates, eds. San Francisco, CA: Jossey-Bass Publishers, pp. 375-408.

Weick, K. E. 1984. "Small Wins: Redefining the Scale of Social Problems," *American Psychologist*, 39(1):40-49.

Weick, K. E. 1985. "Sources of Order in Unorganized Systems: Themes in Recent Organizational Theory," in *Organizational Theory and Inquiry: The Paradigm Revolution*. Y. S. Lincoln, ed. Beverly Hills, CA: SAGE Publications, pp. 106-136.

Wilson, B. L. and T. B. Corcoran. 1988. *Successful Secondary Schools*. Philadelphia, PA: The Falmer Press.

Wise, A. E. 1979. *Legistated Learning*. Berkeley, CA: University of California Press.

Wise, A. E. 1988. "Legislated Learning Revisited," *Phi Delta Kappan*, 69(5):329-333.

Wolcott, H. F. 1985. "On Ethnographic Intent," *Educational Administration Quarterly*, 21(3):187-203.

Wolcott, H. F. 1977. *Teachers Versus Technocrats*. Eugene, OR: University of Oregon, Center for Educational Policy and Management.

Zaltman, G., R. Duncan, and J. Holbek. 1973. *Innovation and Organization*. New York, NY: John Wiley & Sons.

# Index